Studies and documents on cultural policies

For a complete list of titles see page 101

Cultural policy in the People's Republic of China

Letting a hundred flowers blossom

Bai Liu

Unesco

Published in 1983 by the United Nations Educational,
Scientific and Cultural Organization,
7 place de Fontenoy, 75700 Paris
Printed by Imprimerie des Presses Universitaires
de France, Vendôme

ISBN 92-3-102153-2

1394

PO(CHI)

© Unesco 1983
Printed in France

Preface

The purpose of this series is to show how cultural policies are planned and implemented in various Member States.

As cultures differ, so does the approach to them. It is for each Member State to determine its cultural policy and methods according to its own conception of culture, its socio-economic system, political ideology and technical development. However, the methods of cultural policy (like those of general development policy) have certain common problems; these are largely institutional, administrative and financial in nature, and the need has increasingly been stressed for exchanging experiences and information about them. This series, each issue of which follows as far as possible a similar pattern so as to make comparison easier, is mainly concerned with these technical aspects of cultural policy.

In general, the studies deal with the principles and methods of cultural policy, the evaluation of cultural needs, administrative structures and management, planning and financing, the organization of resources, legislation, budgeting, public and private institutions, cultural content in eduiation, cultural autonomy and decentralization, the training of personnel, institutional infrastructures for meeting specific cultural needs, the safeguarding of the cultural heritage, institutions for the dissemination of the arts, international cultural co-operation and other related subjects.

The studies, which cover countries belonging to differing social and economic systems, geographical areas and levels of development, present therefore a wide variety of approaches and methods in cultural policy. Taken as a whole, they can provide guidelines to countries that have yet to establish cultural policies, while all countries, especially those seeking new formulations of such policies, can profit by the experience already gained.

This study was prepared for Unesco by Bai Liu, an art critic, who is also one of the responsible members of *Wenyi Yanjiu* (Research on Literature and Art), a theoretical journal published by the China Art Research Institute. Born in 1934 in the city of Zhenjiang in east China's Jiangsu Province, he is the author of many research papers and articles of literary criticism.

Contents

Foreword

The aim of this monograph is to explain the series of policies that China has formulated to further its socialist culture and to contribute to the development of world culture.

While presenting an up-to-date picture of China's cultural policies, this study mainly describes their impact on China's cultural development and their role in creating a thriving culture. The current situation of cultural planning in China is discussed in conjunction with historical experiences.

The text by Bai Liu, an art critic, was written and edited with the help of the principal cultural departments in China. Contributions were also made by a number of specialists, professors, scholars and translators who either supplied relevant materials or took part in writing some of the chapters.

China Art Research Institute

Introduction

With one of the world's earliest civilizations, China is an inexhaustible treasure-house of culture. It is also a fascinating and mysterious land, abounding in cultural riches that need to be explored for a better understanding of the country. Since the birth of the new China much has been done to expand international cultural exchanges, and good results have been obtained in promoting the understanding of Chinese culture by the people of other countries. Such exchanges, however, were disrupted during the turmoil of the 1966–76 Cultural Revolution and were resumed and developed only after the Gang of Four was toppled. The Chinese Government and people consider the socialist modernization drive to be both patriotic and internationalist in nature. They are devoted to world peace and friendly relations with the people of other countries. Upholding the Five Principles of Peaceful Coexistence and the open-door policy of economic exchanges with other countries, they are working to expand such exchanges and co-operation throughout the world in the economic, cultural, scientific and technological fields. In a spirit of friendship towards all peoples, this monograph attempts to give an outline of cultural development since China entered a new period of history and to furnish an explanation of relevant policies and principles in the hope that it will contribute to cultural interflow between nations.

China's cultural policies and principles

Historical background

Archaeological finds show that there were primitive people living in China as early as 20,000 years ago. China became a slave society during the Xia Dynasty, around 2000 B.C. By the time of the Shang Dynasty (1523–1027 B.C.), the foundations of Chinese culture—including music, art, a written language, literature, the calendar, astronomy, medicine, history and certain branches of science—had already been laid. The development of writing was a major milestone in mankind's cultural progress. Inscriptions on oracular bones and tortoise shells unearthed from the site of the Shang Dynasty's capital (in today's Anyang, Henan Province), which record the political, economic and cultural development as well as social life of the time, bear testimony to the splendid Chinese culture that existed 3,000 years ago. When the slave society developed into a feudal society during the Spring and Autumn and Warring States Periods (770–221 B.C.), various schools of thought and academic groups sprang up throughout the land, and there emerged the flourishing state in which 'prominent scholars vied with one another and a hundred schools of thought contended'. In 221 B.C. Emperor Qin Shihuang (the first emperor of the Qin Dynasty) unified China into a multinational feudal country, and a magnificent culture developed.

For more than 2,000 years after the Qin Dynasty (221–206 B.C.) until the middle of the nineteenth century, China remained a feudal society and was ruled by the following dynasties: the Qin, the Han, the Wei, the Jin, the Southern and Northern, the Sui, the Tang, the Five Dynasties, the Song, the Yuan, the Ming and the Qing. During this long period the Chinese people created one of the world's most splendid cultures. In many respects, however, its origins lay in the culture prior to the Qin Dynasty, which had a tremendous and far-reaching influence on the development of the culture that succeeded it.

11

The Qin Dynasty, which put an end to long years of conflict and hostility between the warring states, played a great role in Chinese history, but because of its policy of tight ideological control it did not greatly advance the culture of the country.

During the 400 years of the Han Dynasty (206 B.C.–A.D. 220), there were many achievements in the fields of literature and art. *Baixi*—including acrobatics, Chinese boxing and swordplay, comic performances, music and dance—was very popular among the people. Because of the importance that the imperial music and dance institution gave to poetry, in particular, it flourished as never before, as did music and dancing. There were also notable developments in architecture and sculpture, mural painting and the arts and crafts, as well as in science and technology.

The period from the Wei and Jin Dynasties to the Southern and Northern Dynasties (A.D. 190–589) was characterized by social turmoil, and this was reflected in the literature and art of that period. A generation of poets came to the fore, represented by Cao Cao and Cao Zhi, who carried on the Han tradition of folk songs and ballads. In their poems they described the chaotic political situation and expressed their aspiration to play a part in bringing about the unification of the country. Thus they fostered a new poetic style, known as the 'style of the Jianan Period'. Under its influence, literary criticism also made much headway. Two masterpieces of literary theory—*Wen Xin Diao Long* (literary critique) and *Shi Ping* (an analysis of poetry)—represented the pinnacle of the classical Chinese theory of literature and art.

This period also saw an increasing interest in metaphysics and in Buddhism. There were at that time more than 30,000 Buddhist monasteries in various parts of the country, some of which are still in existence and are precious examples of Chinese architecture. The Yungang, Dunhuang and Maijishan Grottoes, preserved throughout the dynasties, are treasure-houses containing Buddhist statues and magnificent murals. Calligraphy also flourished at this time, with various styles of writing competing with one another. Wang Xizhi, a celebrated calligrapher of the Eastern Jin Dynasty (A.D. 317–420), developed a style of handwriting whose 'strokes are swift as the drifting clouds and vigorous as an unruly dragon'.

The short-lived Sui Dynasty (518–618) continued the religious and cultural progress of the previous dynasty and made advances in phonology and bibliography.

During the Tang Dynasty (618–907) that followed, China became the most powerful and unified feudal country since the Qin and Han Dynasties. Li Yuan, the founding emperor, and his son Emperor Tai Zhong (Li Shimin) were both capable rulers. They restored social order and revived the economy by instituting the land-equalization system and adopting a series of measures restricting the privileges of bureaucrats and landlords.

During the reign of Emperor Tai Zhong, in particular, political power was consolidated, the feudal economy and culture prospered as never before, and cultural exchanges with other countries expanded on an unprecedented scale. This provided the conditions necessary for the development of traditional Chinese music, dancing, painting, sculpture, calligraphy, novels, prose and poetry. Many famous men of letters and artists came to the fore, and various schools of art vied with each other for prominence.

Poetry flourished under the Tang Dynasty. Some 50,000 poems were written during this period, and there were at least fifty poets of distinction. A number of them were also gifted in painting, calligraphy, music and dancing. Li Bai and Du Fu, who were contemporaries, wrote works that are landmarks in the romantic and realistic schools of Chinese poetry.

Towards the end of the Tang Dynasty power fell into the hands of a few eunuchs, and the country was torn apart by rival military governors. Finally this dynasty crumbled and was replaced by the Five Dynasties and Ten States. After a successful coup d'état in Chenqiao (Kaifeng), Zhao Kuangyin, a general of the later Zhou period (the last of the Five Dynasties), seized power in A.D. 960 and established the Song Dynasty, thereby once again unifying the country.

The rulers of the Song Dynasty (960–1279), who attached great importance to the role of culture in consolidating their political power, did much to train competent people in the trades and professions. Government and private schools sprang up in all the prefectures and counties. The invention of letterpress printing led to the appearance of a great number of publications and encouraged cultural development. Poetry, prose and texts for storytellers (then a budding form of folk literature) all flourished. But above all, it was the golden age of paintings and ci (poetry written with a fixed number of lines and words to certain tunes with strict tonal patterns and rhyme schemes), both of which enriched the fine traditions of Chinese culture.

The Yuan Dynasty (1279–1368), which followed, ushered in a new era of unprecedented national unity, hastened the growth of China as a multinational country and promoted friendly relations between the various nationalities. The importance of using intellectuals to consolidate their regime was understood by the Yuan rulers, and in the process of unifying China they also advocated the rule of law and upheld Confucianism. They set up schools and invited eminent scholars to help run the country. This helped to encourage the growth of feudal literature and art.

The greatest achievement of the Yuan Dynasty in the literary field was zaju, a drama incorporating singing, dialogue and dancing. It developed a unique national style. Texts were written which combined verse and prose, and which became the foundation for the development of the performing arts. The period of the Yuan Dynasty was the golden age of Chinese drama. There were over eighty dramatists of Han and other nationalities in the country, and over 500 works were written. Guan Hanqing, a well-known playwright at that time, wrote over sixty plays,

13

most of which have been lost. His extant masterpieces include *Snow in Midsummer*, *Rescued by a Coquette*, *Butterfly Dream* and *Riverside Pavilion*. Wang Shifu was another famous writer of this period, and his work *The Western Chamber* is well known. The dramas written during the Yuan Dynasty had a far-reaching influence on the culture of the Ming and Qing Dynasties.

The Ming Dynasty (1368–1644) marked the beginning of the decline of China's feudal society. Major cultural achievements during this period included works of fiction and plays. *Romance of the Three Kingdoms* by Luo Guanzhong (1330–1400), *Water Margin* by Shi Naian (1296–1370) and *Pilgrimage to the West* by Wu Chengen (1500–1582), are literary masterpieces based on folk-tales and occupy an important place in the history of Chinese literature.

After the *zaju* of the Yuan Dynasty, drama developed considerably during the late Ming period. Tang Xianzu (1550–1617) was the best-known writer, and his *The Peony Pavilion* is a celebrated romantic work. There were also notable achievements in painting, woodcuts and architecture.

Feudal society ended with the Qing Dynasty, which spanned nearly 300 years from 1644 to 1911. The fiction and drama of the seventeenth and eighteenth centuries were notable. For instance, *Strange Tales from the Carefree Studio*, by Pu Songling (1640–1715), and *The Scholars*, by Wu Jingzi (1701–54), were excellent examples of the short story and satirical genres. *A Dream of Red Mansions*, a world-famous realist work, marks a high point in fiction-writing in China. It has aroused great interest among literary experts, and many research works on it have been written in the past 200 years. *The Palace of Eternal Youth*, by Hong Sheng (1645–1704), and *The Peach-Blossom Fan*, by Kong Shangren (1648–1718), are representative works of drama of this period, in which painting, gardens, handicrafts and architecture also flourished.

In the latter part of the Qing Dynasty, three stages of cultural development can be seen: the movement of enlightenment, the reform movement and the democratic revolution of the bourgeoisie. Anti-imperialism, patriotism and democracy were major aspects of bourgeois culture and created the historical conditions for the further development of China's civilization.

After the Opium War of 1840 China was gradually reduced to the status of a semi-colonial, semi-feudal country. The people waged a heroic and protracted struggle to win independence and democracy. In 1919 the cataclysmic Movement of the 4th May, which stood for ideological emancipation, ushered in the new democratic revolution and exerted a profound influence on both social progress and cultural development. It also paved the way for the founding, in 1921, of the Chinese Communist Party. In the countryside, the revolution gathered momentum, and a mass cultural movement sprang up in the rural revolutionary base areas hand in hand with the Communist-led left-wing literary and art movement in areas under

Kuomintang rule. Lu Xun, the standard-bearer of this movement, made a great contribution to China's revolutionary literature and art. Chairman Mao Zedong, who spoke highly of Lu Xun's work, published his celebrated *Talks at the Yanan Forum on Literature and Art* in 1942. Integrating Marxist-Leninist theories with China's specific conditions, the *Talks* set forth the guiding ideas for revolutionary literature and art and have since had a far-reaching influence. However, as most regions of the country had not been liberated at that time, the people could not become the real masters of their culture. In 1949 the People's Republic of China was established, and one-fourth of the world's population found itself in a new socialist society. A new era began for China's cultural development.

The Chinese nation has existed for 4,000 years. Approximately fifty ethnic groups live within its frontiers, including Hans, Mongolians, Huis, Tibetans, Manchus, Zhuangs, Dais, Uygurs and Gaoshans. Chinese history and culture are remarkable for the unity between these groups. In this big community' the cultures of the various nationalities interact and help to promote each other; at the same time they continually enrich their own heritage with elements from the culture of other countries. Thus China has acquired a unique cultural tradition with distinctive features of its own.

The term 'culture' in ancient China signified 'rule by culture' and 'education through culture'. The feudal rulers of the various dynasties, without exception, made the culture created by the people serve the ruling cliques' own interests and spiritual enjoyment. They used it as an instrument to govern and educate the people. Special government departments were set up to take charge of certain forms of culture in line with the needs of the emperors and their cliques. The academy of music during the Han Dynasty, for instance, was in charge of collecting folk-poems and folk-songs. This enabled them to know what the people thought and said about the government. Another example is the Tang Dynasty's imperial academy and its dancing school, which were responsible for arranging recreational activities for the imperial family. Gradually, with the passage of time, the functions of some of these government cultural institutions were greatly expanded and changed. The imperial academy of the Tang Dynasty, for example, became a place for the emperors of the Ming and Qing Dynasties to meet and train intellectuals for their service, and the power of such institutions, as part of the structure of the central government, extended beyond the imperial court.

It is clear that the people during the various dynasties created the nation's material and cultural wealth and that China's close affinity with them and their democratic outlook was at the heart of its fine cultural tradition. However, the cultural needs of the ruling classes also greatly influenced the development of culture. The main reason why the 'Jianan Literature' between the Eastern Han Dynasty and the Wei Period of the Three Kingdoms, the poetry of the Tang and Song Dynasties, the drama of

15

the Yuan Dynasty, the novels and drama of the Ming and Qing Dynasties and the paintings of various periods, flourished as they did was that they had a solid social foundation and were popular with the people. Moreover, it should not be forgotten that the emperors and their officials liked these art forms especially and made efforts to promote them. Some of the more capable rulers tried to maintain close ties with the people or to express sympathy for them when it was politically expedient or when they met with setbacks in their efforts to achieve control. This fact must be appreciated in order to understand present-day China's policies towards feudal and bourgeois culture.

Just as the culture of each successive period continued the fine traditions and experiences of the past, so the achievements of the new China's socialist culture stem from the development of a rich cultural heritage. To achieve new goals in the interests of the people and in conformity with their aspirations and aesthetic needs is the starting point and ultimate aim of the cultural policies the new China has formulated and is implementing. To be mindful of the lessons of history, to proceed always on the basis of China's actual conditions and to do everything possible to serve the country's 1,000 million people—these are the keys to a comprehensive understanding of China's current cultural policies.

Cultural principles and policies

Socialist China's principles and policies are formulated to help fulfil the specific tasks of a certain period of historical development.

At present, the country's general goal is to unite the people of all national groups in order to develop the socialist economy in a planned manner, to achieve better economic results and to make China a modern, powerful socialist country that is democratic and has a high level of cultural development. This aim represents the people's immediate and long-term interests and is regarded as the general line to be followed in all fields of work (including decisions on, and implementation of, principles and policies). Moreover, it provides a goal ideologically, in practical work, and in the transformation of the objective world. This general aim can also be considered the Chinese people's line of political thought.

The state's general task is embodied in all aspects of the socialist cause. To ensure its fulfilment, the Chinese Communist Party and the People's Government have worked out various principles and policies in the political, economic, military and cultural fields and in foreign relations.

Principles and policies are interrelated and cannot be separated, the former representing the orientation and goal of a cause and the latter the starting point and ultimate aim of practical action. In actual life, doing any job is tantamount to carrying out a certain policy, either consciously or unconsciously.

In practical work, anticipated aims can be achieved only through correct methods and many-sided efforts. To help socialist literature and art to thrive, for example, correct socialist policies and principles should be worked out and implemented, and related questions should be solved, i.e. those concerning economic measures, the quality of literary and artistic creation, cultural facilities, training, the establishment of relevant institutions, and the relationship between quantity and quality. In addition, political and ideological work should be stressed. This has its own principles and policies, and plays a guiding role in all fields of socialist undertaking, including literature and art.

In addition to the specific principles and policies for every field of work decided by the Chinese Communist Party, there are principles that serve as overall guidelines—doing everything for the people, seeking the truth from facts in practical work, practising criticism and self-criticism, unity and education, and letting a hundred flowers blossom and a hundred schools of thought contend in the scientific, literary, artistic and cultural fields.

Socialist modernization at the present stage of historical development aims at a high level of material and cultural development. The latter covers progress in education, science, culture, art, health work and sports, but also, as determined by the socialist system, the orientation and level of development of political ideology, social ethics and moral values. China's socialist cultural undertakings shoulder a heavy responsibility for these two aspects of cultural development.

The Chinese Communist Party and the government attach great importance to the development of these undertakings and consider that they play an indispensable part in the socialist cause. To assist them they have worked out a series of policies, under the principle of democratic centralism, which have in practice proved to be scientific, correct and effective.

'Serving the people, serving socialism' is a guiding principle for any cultural undertaking or work and indicates the direction of development of contemporary Chinese culture. It is also the goal for cultural workers of all nationalities in their united effort to bring about a thriving socialist culture and ethic, and the yardstick for judging the right from the wrong and the good from the bad in practical work.

In the cultural field, to serve the people and to achieve concrete results means to serve the intellectuals, cadres and all those who support socialism and love the motherland, but above all the primary task is to serve the workers, peasants and soldiers of the People's Liberation Army, for they are the main creators of material and cultural wealth and they make up the majority of the population. To serve socialism is to serve the great cause of socialist modernization—i.e. to serve socialist politics, economics, military affairs, culture and other undertakings. This demands that literature and art play a special role, which no other department can play, in satisfying the needs of the people's cultural life, bringing up a new generation of socialist-minded young people and raising society's ideological, cultural and moral

17

levels. At the present time, the government is calling on writers and artists to do their best to reflect the people's great endeavour to achieve socialist modernization, portray the broad vistas of China's reality and depict her rich history. They are also called on to eulogize communist ideas and moral values, patriotism, and revolutionary heroism, so as to help the people understand and overcome obstacles to advancement, fortify their will and confidence and inspire them to work with enthusiasm for 'the four modernizations'.

To carry out the principle of 'serving the people, serving socialism' it is imperative to handle correctly the relationship between cultural workers and those they serve. The people need culture, but culture needs the people even more. Only by consciously identifying themselves with the work to be done and integrating themselves with the people can writers and artists attain their goals. In China the mark of a successful career as a poet, writer or artist lies in links with the public. Such relations enable the creators to acquire the necessary materials concerning the people's life for their creative work and also help them to develop their talent. Their creative life will inevitably suffer if they neglect such contacts. This is a law of art and the way to develop a flourishing socialist literature and art, and it is the reason for saying that the people are the 'mother' of literature and art.

'Let a hundred flowers blossom and a hundred schools of thought contend, weed through the old to bring forth the new, make the past serve the present and foreign things serve China!' These are the principles for correctly understanding and handling all aspects of culture and art, the cultural heritage and foreign culture, science, and technology, and they have opened up broad creative avenues leading to a prosperous socialist culture.

The principle of 'letting a hundred flowers blossom and a hundred schools of thought contend' is widely recognized as expediting the development of socialist science, culture and art. This principle was conceived in the light of China's actual conditions. Based on the understanding that contradictions of various types still exist in a socialist society, it stems from the state's urgent demands for a rapid development of its economy and culture.

To implement this principle in art and literature, the free development of different forms and styles should be encouraged, and in the scientific field discussions and debates between different schools of learning should be advocated. Resorting to administrative measures to compel people to follow one style or one school of thought while banning all others is undoubtedly detrimental to the healthy growth of art and science. The principle of 'letting a hundred flowers blossom and a hundred schools of thought contend' demands that questions of right and wrong in art and science be solved through free discussions and in practice, and not settled in a simplistic and crude manner. In literary and artistic creation, the subject-matter should be multifarious; writers and artists should have full freedom to choose and handle their own themes. So long as their work is

18

beneficial to socialist ethics and to the satisfaction of the people's increasing demand for a rich cultural life, writers and artists can choose subject-matter according to their experience of society and life and their interests and skills. A writer can describe the life of today or of the past; he can choose between comedy and tragedy, and he can praise, criticize or satirize as he wishes. In short, the writer has the freedom to decide what and how to write, and an artist can choose what to portray or reflect, provided that they each depict life or history correctly. Different styles and genres in literature and art should have the freedom to develop and compete with each other; creativity is thus encouraged.

The principle of 'letting a hundred flowers blossom and a hundred schools of thought contend' is an important one, and leaders at all levels should uphold it in their day-to-day work. The Chinese Government follows this principle in order to give full scope to socialist democracy in literature, art and science. This policy also provides the freedom needed by intellectuals (who are part of the labouring people) to create literature and art and to do scientific research work, and it supports and encourages them in breaking new ground. When people make mistakes they are given the opportunity to correct them, and those who err have the chance to start anew. Under this policy, nobody is allowed to seize on the errors of others, to attack them wilfully, or to punish them indiscriminately.

The leadership at all levels is not allowed to make political charges against any work of literature or art, academic view, artist or scientist. The aim is to open more avenues for cultural growth, the free expression of views and the training of talented people—all for the growth of a culture in the interests of the masses.

Criticism and self-criticism are essential to the development of socialist democracy, stability and unity in socialist society and the correct implementation of the principle of 'letting a hundred flowers blossom and a hundred schools of thought contend'. Facts and reasoning are relied upon to solve ideological questions; criticism, counter-criticism and differing views are allowed, and everyone is expected to uphold the truth and correct mistakes.

This 'two-hundred' principle is based on the people's interests. The People's Republic of China guarantees that the people enjoy their lawful rights in cultural life and the cultural workers their legitimate rights and interests according to law. Citizens of all nationalities in the country have equal rights in the cultural field, and special care and material support are granted to cultural development among the minority nationalities. Women enjoy equal rights with men in all fields of cultural life. Particular attention is paid to enriching the cultural life of children, young people and women. Socialist democracy is inseparable from the socialist legal system. Socialist collectivism provides the universal moral norm for actual life. Individual and collective interests are identical under the socialist system. Should any contradiction arise between one's personal interests and that of the collective, one should consciously subordinate one's own interests to those of the collective. In actual fact, it is imperative to curb and eliminate the various ideologies of the exploiting classes and all other ideas that clash with the socialist system. These include corruption by bourgeois ideas, lingering feudal ideas, anarchism, extreme individualism and bureaucratism. It is also imperative to oppose and crack down on law-breaking activities aimed at scuttling the socialist economy and other socialist undertakings. In the ideological and cultural fields, the principle of 'letting a hundred flowers blossom and a hundred schools of thought contend' should not be interpreted to mean that the interests of the people and the state can be ignored, for they are fundamental. If one were to abandon or shift from this standpoint one would be interpreting this principle to mean bourgeois liberalization, which obviously runs completely counter to the very essence of the principle.

The principle of 'letting a hundred flowers blossom and weeding through the old to bring forth the new' aims to transform China's theatrical arts which are 800 years old. During this long period a considerable number of operas and a rich repertoire were created. Many of the theatrical works faithfully depict history, social life, heroes, patriots, fighters for freedom and the beauty of life in an artistic manner. They extol the ideals and aspirations of the people. They have become a part of the people's cultural life. At the same time, a wealth of experience has accumulated. In playwriting and the performing arts, including singing and acting, expressive techniques and distinctive national styles have developed and are much loved by the people.

China's traditional theatrical arts have made an immense contribution to world civilization. However, because they developed in a feudal society, they were unavoidably influenced by the ideology of the ruling classes, and are a mixture of democratic cream and despotic dregs. Many works contain elements that are feudal, superstitious, eerie or pornographic. How, then, can they be made to serve socialism and the people and contribute to mankind's cultural development?

In the transformation of the drama, the principle of 'letting a hundred flowers blossom and weeding through the old to bring forth the new' calls for criticism of the cultural inheritance, and change and creation based upon it. Thus, China can rid itself of these despotic dregs, retain the democratic essence, and differentiate between the old ruling classes' feudal influence on drama and the elements created by the people—elements that have a close affinity with democracy. It is only in this way that the fine traditions of China's theatrical heritage can be continued and transformed.

Transformation and creation are based on criticizing the cultural heritage and on correct viewpoints and methods. The wisdom of contemporary people is needed to enrich traditional theatre, revitalize ancient forms of art, help them develop under the new conditions, and make them compatible with the ideology of today and new experiences in culture and art. Thus the old can be made to serve the new (i.e. the ancient forms of art can be made to serve the needs of the people by portraying the real, colourful life of today).

In compiling and re-editing traditional theatrical works or writing works with historical themes, criticism of the cultural heritage, its transformation and creation must not be mechanically separated; they form a harmonious process.

Guided by the principle of 'letting a hundred flowers blossom and weeding through the old to bring forth the new', fruitful results have been achieved. Statistics show that by April 1957 over 51,000 traditional theatrical items had been collected and 4,200 others had been re-edited and improved. Many outstanding pieces are now in the repertoire, and opera genres that were on the verge of extinction in the old China and traditional art techniques have gained new vitality. The opera form called *Kunqu*, for example, was dying out, but after the People's Republic was founded it was revived with the staging of the artistically refurbished *Fifteen Strings of Cash*. This production has become the talk of China's theatrical world. In actual fact, it was not the presentation of this opera that saved *Kunqu*, but the principle of 'weeding through the old to bring forth the new'. Today China has more than 300 opera genres. Traditional operas and works with historical and contemporary themes have appeared in large numbers. The various schools are blossoming and vying with each other, and numerous 'new buds' have appeared.

The principle has also stimulated the transformation and development of the folk culture and art of the various nationalities. Many works of folk art have been recorded, compiled, re-edited and popularized, and this has in turn encouraged the creation and staging of items in different forms and with various themes. This has given a distinctive national flavour to China's culture, helped popularize it among the people and enabled the art of the minorities to grow rapidly.

The principle of 'making the past serve the present and foreign things serve China' scientifically governs the relationship between China's own culture and that of foreign countries, bourgeois and feudal cultures included. Present-day culture is established and developed on the basis of the world's fine cultural heritage. To build a new socialist culture, it is necessary to draw upon the cream of China's cultural heritage and on the progressive culture and outstanding legacy of foreign countries. The criterion is whether such cultures are beneficial to the people and whether they are of progressive historical significance. Each case is handled on its merits. However, the work of carrying forward China's cultural heritage and learning from foreign culture should on no account supersede the creation of a new socialist culture. In this respect, both national nihilism and the outdated tendency to regard everything in China's past as good should be opposed; both blind faith in things foreign and big-nation chauvinism and cultural despotism should be opposed.

'Making the past serve the present' means that China inherits its cultural heritage for the purpose of promoting the building of a new culture to meet the people's needs. A splendid culture was created in the country's long years of feudalism. To carry forward this rich heritage is a necessary condition for developing a new national culture and enhancing national self-confidence. In practice, China is opposed to the negation of everything foreign and to extolling the past to the neglect of the present. The correct attitude should be to get rid of 'dregs' and absorb the 'essence', rather than swallow everything without making any criticism.

'Making foreign things serve China' means that in developing the country's new national culture it is necessary to draw on the progressive culture and fine cultural heritage of foreign countries. It is wrong to be isolated from the outside world and oppose everything from abroad. China is also opposed to mechanically copying and imitating foreign culture without making any critical analyses. The correct attitude should be to learn from and absorb foreign culture so that it serves the actual needs of the Chinese people, to incorporate its strong points and make them part of the national culture.

Guided by the principle of 'making the past serve the present and foreign things serve China', the nation's socialist culture has been developing vigorously and fruitful results have been obtained. This important cultural policy also applies to the social and natural sciences.

China's cultural undertakings also follow the principle of 'combining popularization with elevation', which shows how to serve the masses now that the orientation of 'doing everything for the people' has been clearly defined. It also embodies the mass line—a fine revolutionary tradition—in the cultural field.

In the old China, workers, peasants and other labouring people were not only subject to political oppression and economic exploitation but were also deprived of the right to receive an education and enjoy a cultural life. The result was that most of them remained poor, illiterate and backward. They were emancipated politically and economically after the birth of the new China. As their own masters, they have the urgent desire to be liberated culturally and to be the masters of culture, as well. Because of this, the cultural principle of 'combining popularization with elevation' was laid down. Popularization means disseminating cultural knowledge among the people, primarily the workers, peasants and soldiers; 'elevation' means raising culture to a new level through this popularization. Such 'elevation' is conditioned by 'popularization', while at the same time it gives guidance to popularization.

Popularizing cultural knowledge demands that the intellectual food we provide for the people should meet their needs and be easily accepted by them. Literature and art, for example, should be created to suit their ideological and cultural levels.

'Popularization' and 'elevation' condition, supplement and promote each other; the former is aimed at creating the conditions for the latter.

Without popularization, elevation will have no foundation, and without elevation, we will always remain at the same level and popularization will lose its significance. The two aspects involve both the people served by culture and the cultural work itself. The level and result of the work of 'popularization' and 'elevation', whether quantitatively or qualitatively, are accompanied by the steady raising of the people's scientific and cultural levels and the steady progress of cultural undertakings as a whole.

In the thirty-four years since the establishment of the People's Republic, cultural work among the people has progressed apace under this policy. Scientific and cultural knowledge has been widely popularized among the worker-peasant-soldier masses, and their ability and level of artistic appreciation have been raised conspicuously. It is particularly heartening that historic changes have taken place in the ranks of the intellectuals, who account for 3 per cent of the total population. Ninety per cent of them have been trained in the new China. The socialist cause depends in a large measure upon them. Many outstanding people have been trained in the scientific, cultural, artistic and educational fields and have become scientists, artists, men of letters, educationalists, theoreticians and statesmen respected by the people.

The foregoing brief discussion shows that the principles and policies of the Communist Party and the government concerning cultural undertakings all have the same purpose—the fulfilment of the state's general tasks for the new period of historical development. They are interrelated, and their relationship is not one of mutual exclusion but of interaction and mutual promotion.

The guideline for correctly implementing cultural principles and policies

Our experiences, both positive and negative, in the last thirty-four years since the birth of the new China have proved the correctness of the Chinese Communist Party's cultural principles and policies. But practice also shows that the presence of correct principles and policies does not mean that every field of practical work is done correctly and the desired results obtained. The mistakes that have been made, both in the guiding ideas and in practical work, have brought setbacks and losses to the socialist cultural cause. In the Cultural Revolution, in particular, the rampant Lin Biao and Jiang Qing counter-revolutionary cliques brought grave destruction to this cause. This does not mean, however, that these socialist cultural principles and policies were wrong. Mistakes in guiding ideas (mostly 'leftist' mistakes) prevented us from correctly implementing these principles and policies. Moreover, the errors had much to do with sabotage by the Lin Biao and Jiang Qing cliques, who did their utmost to distort and tamper with these principles and policies. The mistakes committed were different in essence from sabotage by these political swindlers.

23

In the administration of cultural affairs, obtaining satisfactory results from a correct principle or policy depends directly on the following factors: (a) correctness of the ideas of the executants, (b) their professional ability, judgement and understanding of the principles and policies, and (c) whether they base their work on facts or whether they work subjectively and dogmatically. An example is the implementation of China's policy concerning national regional autonomy and the relations between the different nationalities. Only by proceeding from the actual conditions in the areas inhabited by minority nationalities can the socialist principles and policies be correctly implemented. On the other hand, because the conditions of life are constantly changing, it is necessary to revise some policies accordingly. Basing itself on experiences gained in leading the revolution, particularly the lessons drawn from the Cultural Revolution, and taking into account the situation that has arisen since China entered the new period of historical development, the Communist Party has reaffirmed the ideological line of understanding the objective world in a scientific way and correctly handling problems and the four basic principles that should be followed in various fields of endeavour.

The ideological line is to proceed in all cases from reality, integrate theory with practice, seek the truth from facts, test and develop the truth in practice.

The four basic principles are to uphold the socialist road, the people's democratic dictatorship (i.e. the proletarian dictatorship), the leadership of the Communist Party, and Marxism-Leninism and Mao Zedong thought.

These four basic principles constitute the political foundation for the unity of all the nationalities in China; they have also been written into the draft of the revised Constitution as the fundamental guarantee for the smooth progress of the modernization programme. The most important point in these four principles is to uphold the leadership of the Chinese Communist Party. Without it, there would have been no new China and there could be no modernized socialist China. Party leadership depends mainly on the correctness of the party's ideological and political direction and its line, principles and policies. The Chinese Communist Party is the faithful representative of the people of all nationalities in China and the guide in all fields of endeavour. It is not a demigod, however. In the great cause of transforming Chinese society the party cannot avoid making some mistakes. Its great strength lies not in freeing itself from mistakes, but in the fact that it can overcome shortcomings, correct mistakes, surmount all hardships and finally attain its goals. Party leadership and activities in state political life are all carried out within the framework of the Constitution and state law. The party's views are identical with the aspirations of the people and therefore every honest and upright Chinese supports its leadership. Words and deeds that weaken, bypass or sabotage this leadership are detrimental to the Chinese people's interests and will and therefore cannot be tolerated.

The party's ideological line of seeking the truth from facts is the most fundamental ideological and working method for correctly upholding the four basic principles. Upholding the party's ideological line and adhering to the four basic principles is China's method of correctly carrying out the various principles and policies concerning its socialist cultural undertakings.

Administrative structure
and management
of China's cultural undertakings

Form and content
of the administrative structure

China's cultural undertakings include literature and art, the press, radio and television, education, physical culture and sports, health work, enhancement of the cultural heritage, and publications. They involve philosophy and the social and natural sciences. In the management of various fields of cultural work there are appropriate government cultural institutions at the central and local levels, and national as well as local people's cultural groups and organizations.

To ensure the healthy development of the work under their jurisdiction, the government cultural institutions at the central level hold themselves responsible to the country and the people. When carrying out cultural principles and policies, they ensure that they proceed from reality in drawing up concrete programmes, and they formulate the necessary rules and regulations for drama and films, television and radio, music and dancing, the fine arts, education and sports, the protection of the cultural heritage, museums and libraries, publications, parks and gardens, the protection of rare animals and plants, and other cultural work and important cultural facilities. This is all to ensure the implementation of the state's general cultural principles and policies. Local government cultural administrative institutions at various levels also have the right to enact their own rules and regulations and detailed measures for the management of cultural undertakings in the light of local conditions.

The central cultural administrative institutions give guidance in the management of cultural affairs to local cultural administrative institutions (provincial, municipal, autonomous regional and county). These institutions are led by the party committees and government departments at various levels. Leading party and government departments of all grades are duty-bound to show concern for, and give support to, the development of culture in the country.

The People's Republic of China is a multinational socialist country with a large population covering a vast area. In the management of cultural undertakings, the various central cultural administrative institutions and equivalent local administrative organs, as well as the people's cultural organizations at the same level, work in close co-operation. Their status is equal, and they have the same objectives and general tasks. It is precisely through such co-operation that favourable conditions are often created for the development of their work. It is natural, therefore, that whenever a department proposes a cultural action of great significance, it has the whole-hearted support of all departments concerned. For example, in order to strengthen education among young people, there is a movement called Learn from Lei Feng (a nationally known selfless fighter). Students strive to be triply good (good in ideology, study and health) and foster new social ethics. The movement was launched among primary-school and middle-school students and has won the support of government cultural departments, the Communist Youth League, the trade unions, women's federations and other popular organizations because it is not associated only with educational departments. When supplying youth with intellectual food, cultural departments provide items and performances which young people like, such as literary works, films, drama, music and the fine arts; in addition, they give financial help by reducing charges or suppressing them altogether. They also provide subsidies and material rewards (according to policies) to art troupes and film-projection units that perform or give special shows for young people. Thanks to the care shown by the government, a national children's work committee has been set up, which is responsible for co-ordinating the organization of cultural and arts activities for children, providing them with goods in daily use and expanding nurseries and kindergartens. As regards other aspects of the cultural undertakings, there is harmonious co-operation in practical work no matter whether there are special co-ordinating organizations or not. Sometimes contradictions between departments may arise, but they are always solved through consultation. To promote the development of cultural undertakings, co-ordinated action is being taken by the central government cultural institutions in conjunction with the local institutions concerned, and by the popular cultural organizations alone, or with government organizations. These actions are usually decided on through joint meetings or specialized discussions and by working out together the relevant documents before putting them into practice.

The administrative organizations in charge of China's cultural policies are discussed in the following sections.

GOVERNMENT ORGANIZATIONS

The Ministry of Culture, the Ministry of Education, the Chinese Academy of Social Sciences, the Ministry of Radio and Television, the Xinhua News Agency, the State Physical Culture and Sports Commission, and the

Committee for Reforming the Chinese Written Language are all government organizations in charge of cultural undertakings under the State Council. They are also administrative organs responsible for the implementation of the nation's cultural policies in accordance with their specialized fields and division of labour. Corresponding local government cultural organizations are set up in the various provinces, municipalities, autonomous regions, prefectures and counties throughout the country.

The scope of administration of these organizations is defined according to the contents of their particular undertakings, and they have evolved their own management systems in the course of practice. These will not be dealt with in detail here, but we shall, as an example, deal with the management system of the Ministry of Culture, to show how China's cultural undertakings are managed—i.e. the administrative structure in charge of cultural policies.

The Ministry of Culture is an administrative organ responsible for the nation's cultural policies. It has under its authority about a dozen departments and bureaux in charge of the arts, films, publications, cultural heritage, art education, the culture of minority nationalities, mass culture, children's arts, libraries, cultural exchanges with foreign countries, planned financial affairs and personnel. The names of these organizations give an idea of the scope of their management. Viewed from the subjective angle of the management of cultural undertakings, the aim in setting up these organizations is to meet the needs of the development of culture. But since objective reality is constantly changing and developing, appropriate readjustments are necessary in order to keep pace with the development of socialist cultural undertakings. This is why there are occasional changes in these organizations, which is a normal phenomenon.

The tasks of the Ministry of Culture with regard to the management of cultural undertakings are to give guidance for professional work in accordance with relevant principles and policies, to adopt diverse measures to encourage literary and artistic creation and promote artistic production, to work out an overall plan for developing socialist cultural undertakings and achieve a comprehensive balance, to engage in investigation and study and sum up experiences gained, to show concern for mass cultural undertakings, to give due importance to the development of the culture and art of national minorities, to discover and train talented writers and artists, to raise constantly the ideological level and professional skills of the literary and art contingents, to strengthen literary criticism and promote the study of literary and artistic theories and of culture, science and technology, to organize actively and develop international cultural exchanges, to strengthen ideological and political work, to unite with all the forces possible to make appropriate contributions to the development and flourishing of culture and to the building of socialist ethics and cultural civilization.

Cultural bureaux (or sections) are set up in the government organizations at provincial, municipal, autonomous regional, prefectural (i.e. an administrative agency of a province stationed in a prefecture) and county levels. Their main tasks are to implement socialist cultural principles and policies, accept the guidance of the cultural departments at the higher levels, manage cultural undertakings in the light of local conditions, draw up plans and detailed implementation regulations for the development of cultural undertakings, and organize and carry out various kinds of cultural work.

PEOPLE'S ORGANIZATIONS

The forerunner of the China Federation of Literary and Art Circles was the All-China Federation of Literary and Art Circles, founded in July 1949 at the All-China Literary and Art Workers' Congress. It was given its present name at the Second National Literary and Art Workers' Congress in September 1953. Its tasks in the new period are to mobilize the nation's writers and artists to strive together for the flourishing of socialist literary and artistic creation so as to enrich the people's cultural life, enhance their mental vision, train new socialist human beings and encourage them to work for the building of a modern socialist motherland; to strengthen cultural exchanges with other countries and develop friendly contacts with writers and artists of various countries; to promote understanding and friendship between the people of China and other countries; and to unite with the people of all countries in the struggle against imperialism, colonialism and hegemonism and in the defence of world peace.

The federation is a union of various literary and art associations, which include the Chinese Writers' Association, the Chinese Musicians' Association, the Chinese Film Workers' Association, the Chinese Dramatists' Association, the Chinese Dancers' Association, the Chinese Ballad Singers' Association, the Chinese Artists' Association, the Chinese Calligraphers' Association, the China Society for the Study of Folk Literature and Art, the Chinese Photographers' Society, and the Chinese Acrobats' Association. All these associations are people's cultural organizations.

All the provinces (except Taiwan), municipalities, autonomous regions and prefectures have, in the light of the development of literature and art in their localities, set up corresponding associations and their own federations as well. In view of the conditions in China today, branch associations are set up only in cities under the direct jurisdiction of some provincial (or autonomous regional) governments. Where conditions are not ripe, literary federations only are established, which exercise functions and powers on behalf of the associations (i.e. recruiting new members). As regards the prefectures, generally speaking only literary federations are set up, and there are no branch associations. Prefectural literary federations are responsible for recruiting new members in places at or below prefectural level. Local associations at various levels are branches of the nation's associations; and national associations and local literary federations and

29

their branches at various levels are all members of the China Federation of Literary and Art Circles. The statutes of the federation and various associations stipulate that national and local literary federations and associations should, by various means, unite with all organizations or individuals who are willing to serve the motherland and the people. Anyone with special professional talent in a certain field of literature and art and anyone who has made contributions should be accepted as a member by the association concerned when he or she applies for membership. According to incomplete statistics, the China Federation of Literary and Art Circles embraces forty member organizations all over the country, and the various associations have accepted 17,740 individuals as members (not including members of local branches). The various associations under the federation have the responsibility to protect their members' creative labour and their legitimate rights and interests.

The China Federation of Literary and Art Circles gives vocational guidance to, and works in co-operation with, the various associations and local literary federations and their branches. The various associations also work in co-operation, and the local literary federations at various levels also give professional guidance to, and co-operate with, their branches. Of course, the various branches also co-operate with each other.

The federation and various associations are organizations in charge of specialized work, and they are non-profit-making people's cultural organizations. They work in close co-ordination with government cultural departments, trade unions, Communist Youth League organizations, women's federations and other popular organizations for the development and prosperity of socialist cultural undertakings.

ORGANIZATIONS IN CHARGE OF CULTURAL EXCHANGE WITH FOREIGN COUNTRIES

The Ministry of Culture is a government institution under the State Council, and is in charge of the nation's cultural exchanges with foreign countries. It has a bureau which handles such exchanges and implements the principles and policies governing them. It acts on behalf of the government in signing cultural agreements, annual implementation plans and plans concerning cultural-exchange items. In addition, it deals with matters concerning contacts and negotiations with foreign countries.

China's cultural policy towards foreign countries is, on the basis of the Five Principles of Peaceful Coexistence, to develop international cultural exchanges, promote friendly contacts with the people of various countries, oppose imperialism, colonialism and hegemony and defend world peace. The Chinese Government attaches great importance to promoting cultural exchanges and co-operation with other countries, particularly the Third World and friendly countries. While learning about all that is useful in foreign culture, it also introduces China's traditional and fine modern culture to the people of other countries. It maintains that all nations have their cultural and artistic treasures and have a contribution to make to the progress of human culture.

Academic studies and exchanges at government-to-government level in literature and art, sports, education, journalism, television and radio and other fields are all under the responsibility of the Ministry of Culture, the Chinese Academy of Social Sciences, the State Commission of Physical Culture and Sports, the Ministry of Education and related government departments.

People's organizations engaged in international cultural exchanges include the Chinese People's Association for Friendship with Foreign Countries, the China Federation of Literary and Art Circles and the various associations. Government organizations in charge of cultural exchanges work in co-operation with them in developing cultural exchanges with the cultural circles, and friendly organizations and personalities of other countries.

The cultural offices and officials of Chinese embassies and consulates carry out their work under the guidance of the ambassadors, and act on behalf of government and people's cultural organizations in arranging exchanges and in co-operation and negotiations with similar organizations in the countries concerned, in order to promote cultural contacts.

RESEARCH INSTITUTES
FOR CULTURAL DEVELOPMENT

Special cultural research organizations have been set up in China. These include the Archaeological Research Institute, the Ancient Documents Research Office, the Literary Research Institute, and institutes of research work on films, drama, the fine arts and the dance. In addition to these government organizations, other research organizations on cultural development have been established by the government and the people themselves at central, provincial, autonomous regional and prefectural levels. Apart from these, there are institutes of higher learning, art institutes and major art performing troupes, all of which have special structures for research on cultural development. They all have their own facilities (libraries or reading rooms) for providing research materials. Their professional work encompasses literature, drama, music, dancing, the fine arts, films, television and radio, publications, cultural-heritage protection, culture, science and technology, library management, the discovery and indexing of traditional arts, and the cultural and artistic development of minority nationalities. They conduct special and comprehensive studies of relevant legislation (including literary and artistic principles and policies) and theories (past and present) according to their specialized fields. The results of their research are of great value to the government and to people's cultural organizations in guiding the development of culture and conducting cultural activities, to writers and artists in their creative work, for the correct appreciation and continuation of the cultural heritage, and for raising the cultural and artistic level and building a new socialist culture.

Government research institutions engaged specially in the study of literature and art are affiliated with the Ministry of Culture or the Chinese Academy of Social Sciences. In the former case, emphasis is laid on research in the arts, while the latter stresses research work on literature.

Institutes under the Ministry of Culture

The Chinese Art Research Institute is a comprehensive multidiscipline art-research institution directly under the Ministry of Culture. Its predecessor was the Literary and Art Research Institute, which was founded in 1975. It was renamed the Chinese Art Research Institute in 1980. It has more than 500 staff members, of whom 80 per cent are researchers and assistant research workers. It consists of research organizations or research departments (corresponding to research institutes) specializing in the study of operas, modern plays, music, the fine arts, films, the dance, the classical novel *Dream of the Red Mansion*, contemporary literature and art, and foreign literature and art. It also has a cultural and arts publishing house serving literary and art research work and publishing the results of research as well as well-known literary and art works, both Chinese and foreign, ancient and modern. It has a library of a comprehensive nature, with a rich collection of books, documents, recorded material and statistics. Specialized reading rooms are also set up under various specialized research institutes (or departments).

Literary and Art Studies, edited and published by this institute, is a comprehensive theoretical journal. In addition, the various research institutes (or departments) also publish their own journals and books.

To expand the ranks of people devoted to the study of literary and art theories and to train personnel with Ph.D. and M.A. degrees, the institute has a department for training postgraduates. The first group of such students graduated in the spring of 1982.

Art-research institutes are also established by the cultural bureaux (except those in some areas in Tibet) in the nation's twenty-nine provinces (except Taiwan), municipalities and autonomous regions. The Chinese Art Research Institute has vocational co-operative relations with them.

In addition, in the field of cultural, scientific and technological studies, there are the Chinese Cinematography Institute and the Chinese Theatrical Research Institute directly under the Ministry of Culture. Their objective is to improve the scientific and technological level of the film industry and the theatrical arts, and their research items are included in the state plan. Professionally, they have co-operative relations with the nation's scientific research institutions.

32

Institutes under the Chinese Academy
of Social Sciences

The Chinese Academy of Social Sciences grew out of the Philosophy and Social Sciences Department attached to the Chinese Academy of Sciences. Following the founding of the People's Republic of China in 1949, the Chinese Academy of Sciences set up many research institutes in the fields of natural sciences, philosophy and social sciences. In 1977, the Philosophy and Social Sciences Department was separated from the Chinese Academy of Sciences and became the Chinese Academy of Social Sciences. It has twenty-five research institutes specializing in literature, history, politics, economics, philosophy (including aesthetics), languages, religion and journalism. In addition, under the Chinese Academy of Social Sciences, there are eighty-three social-science research academies or research institutes, specializing in subjects such as literature and art, in the nation's twenty-nine provinces, municipalities and autonomous regions. The Chinese Academy of Social Sciences gives guidance and works in co-operation with these local research institutions.

The Chinese Academy of Social Sciences has under it a publishing house and publishes more than thirty academic journals.

The following is a brief account of the Literary Research Institute and the Foreign Literature Research Institute, both affiliated to the Chinese Academy of Social Sciences.

The Literary Research Institute, set up in 1952, has 250 staff members, 90 per cent of whom are researchers and assistant research workers. The institute has under it a number of departments, engaged in the study of literary and artistic theories, the study of the great writer Lu Xun, and the study of contemporary, modern, ancient, and folk literature. Each department has a library of its own. The institute publishes two journals: *Literary Review* and *Literary Legacy*.

The Foreign Literature Research Institute, set up in 1964, has 180 staff members, 72 per cent of whom are researchers and assistant research workers. The institute has set up six foreign-literature research departments, according to the different language groups and regions, each with a library of its own. The institute publishes two journals: *World Literature* and *Collection of Materials on Foreign Literature*.

MASS-CULTURE ESTABLISHMENTS

Mass-culture undertakings (including those of minority nationalities) occupy an important place in China's cultural policies.

As far as organizations in charge of cultural policies are concerned, the Ministry of Culture has under it a bureau in charge of mass-culture activities and a department in charge of the culture of minority nationalities. Government cultural institutions at the provincial (except Taiwan), municipal, autonomous regional, prefectural and county levels all have their mass-culture departments (or sections), which are responsible for organizing and guiding the people's cultural activities. The main tasks of government organizations in charge of mass-culture activities are to supervise and examine the implementation of cultural principles and policies in various localities, to draw up annual and long-term plans for mass-culture work, to formulate the rules and regulations for halls, centres and mass-art galleries, to commend typical and exemplary cases, to sum up and exchange experiences, and to commend and award advanced collectives and individuals who have distinguished themselves in mass-culture work and promote the development of mass-culture activities as a whole.

As regards cultural facilities, there are mass-art galleries in the various provinces, municipalities, autonomous regions and prefectures. In the counties, people's communes and neighbourhood committees, there are cultural halls and centres, and the factories, rural production brigades and grass-roots army units have recreation centres, cultural and reading rooms. In the cities, whatever their size, there are cultural and youth palaces, palaces for children, and recreation centres. The state plan for expanding cultural activities envisages the gradual development of thousands of towns throughout the country into political, economic and cultural centres for their areas. Initial results have been achieved in the past two years towards this end. Many country towns have built simple cinemas, theatres, book centres, cultural centres, reading rooms and other recreational facilities by relying primarily on the collective economic strength.

TABLE 1. The nation's mass-culture establishments in 1981, excluding amateur mass-creative works and spare-time amateur troupes

Establishments	Cultural departments		Factories, mines and other depart-ments	Collective management
	Number	At county level and below		
Libraries, 1 787	1 787	1 544	—	—
Galleries, 257	256	—	1	—
Halls, 2 893	2 887	2 759	6	—
Centres, 28 417	4 240	4 231	137	24 040
Undertakings, 6 409	4 015	2 368	569	1 825
art troupes, 3 483	2 156	1 258	12	1 315
art centres, 2 302	1,263	845	554	485
Film services, 134 730	15 920	14 061	34 543	84 267
including projection teams, 107 001[1]	7 973	7 798	17 080	81 948

1. Film-projection teams are mass-culture set-ups that move from place to place giving film shows for people in the factories, mines, army units and the vast rural areas.

There are now 257 mass-art galleries, 2,893 cultural halls and over 100,000 film-projection teams in the country; 2,397 performing-art troupes, 28,417 cultural centres, 29,353 amateur mass literary creative groups (27,483 are in the rural areas), 75,616 amateur mass performing groups (64,868 are in the rural areas) at county level or below. Table 1 presents the nation's mass-culture establishments in 1981.

Rapid progress has been made in recent years in developing cultural undertakings among the minority nationalities as a result of the care shown by the People's Government. The population of minority nationalities constitutes only about 6 per cent of the nation's total, but their cultural and art institutions make up about 17 per cent of the country's total. There are 24,267 cultural organizations of various kinds in the national autonomous areas, including 19,820 film-projection units, 602 performing-art troupes, 582 cultural halls, 331 libraries, 2,854 cultural centres and 78 other cultural facilities. Table 2 presents the cultural establishments in the national autonomous areas in 1981. Table 3 lists the nation's literary and art journals.

TABLE 2. Cultural establishments in the national autonomous areas in 1981

Total[1]	Film services[2]			Art undertakings		Mass/culture		
	Cinemas	Theatres	Projection teams	Troupes	Theatres	Libraries	Halls	Centres
24 267	657	187	18 976	602	78	331	582	2 854

1. The statistics do not include amateur mass-creative works and spare-time mass performances.
2. Films are shown mainly in the recreation centres or auditoriums of factories, mines and army units by projection teams, while in the rural areas they are shown mostly in the open air at night. In some places there are simple cinemas and halls for showing films.

TABLE 3. The nation's 437 literary and art journals in 1981

Type	Number	Type	Number
Literary and artistic theory	25	Dancing	4
Literature	211	Photography	3
Films	30	Pictorial	21
Television	2	Ballads	4
Drama	29	Children's literature, art	28
Music	32	Foreign literature, art	16
Fine arts	24	Others	8

Set-up of China's cultural organizations

Socialist China has abolished the system of exploitation of man by man. There are basically two types of ownership of the means of production: socialist ownership by the whole people and socialist collective ownership by the labouring people. The state sector of the economy—i.e. the economy owned by the people—holds the dominant position. Material guarantees for the development of socialist cultural undertakings are provided primarily by the socialist economic sector owned by the whole people (i.e. by the state) and partially by the collective economy. State cultural organizations are affiliated to different departments because they receive funds from different channels. At present, China's cultural establishments belong to the three systems listed below.

ESTABLISHMENTS
UNDER THE MINISTRY OF CULTURE

These include film studios, performing-arts troupes and art-education institutions. All cultural organizations owned by the people and managed by government cultural institutions at various levels are called cultural departments.

ORGANIZATIONS
UNDER OTHER MINISTRIES
AND COMMISSIONS

These include performing-arts bodies such as the railway arts troupe, coal mines arts troupe, film-projection units, literary and art research organizations, radio and television departments, and army literary and art units.

COLLECTIVELY MANAGED ORGANIZATIONS

These include mainly some county performing-arts troupes, cultural centres and commune-run film-projection teams. Their staff members are not on the state's payroll. Those who cannot support themselves receive subsidies from the state and financial aid from society.

In the management of cultural undertakings, in principle, government cultural organizations at central and local levels give professional guidance to, and maintain professional co-operation with, cultural units belonging to different systems. At the same time the cultural organizations under the different systems are under the leadership of the departments concerned in their respective systems. For example, according to statistics released at the end of 1981, there were in the whole country 134,730 film organizations (including studios, distribution companies, projection teams and film-industry departments), 6,409 art organizations (including art creation and research units, performing-arts troupes, exhibition units and performing-art centres), 1,787 libraries, 31,595 mass-culture establishments (including mass-art galleries, cultural halls, cultural centres, and mass-art troupes), 231 art-education organizations, 214 publishing houses, 106 radio stations, 38 television stations, and 2,560 broadcasting relay stations.

With the continuing drive for modernization, the situation is excellent for developing cultural undertakings. To keep pace with this drive, it is necessary to solve the new problems that have arisen and constantly improve the management and raise the work efficiency of cultural undertakings.

System of financial management of China's cultural undertakings

In the new period of socialist modernization, China has adopted the general principle of readjusting, restructuring, consolidating and improving the national economy. Guided by this principle, the state instituted in 1980 the system of allowing state organizations at provincial, municipal and autonomous regional levels to have their own budgets and to be responsible for their own revenue and expenditure. The basic principle is as follows: in order to consolidate the central government's unified leadership and plans and guarantee it the necessary funds, the rights of local financial departments at various levels are clearly defined, and they must also perform their duties. The institution of this system has stimulated the initiative of local authorities and put an end to a situation where 'all eat from the same big pot', irrespective of the amount and quality of the work done.

MANAGEMENT OF BUDGET OF CULTURAL UNDERTAKINGS

The above system is embodied in the financial management of cultural undertakings. With regard to the funds for cultural departments and administrative and management organizations which are owned by the people, the state adopts the method of 'letting them fulfil their tasks with the funds specified in the budget' (i.e. the state provides the funds they need—wages and expenses for various activities). This method takes two different forms according to the conditions in the various cultural departments, i.e. management of total budget funds (all the funds are provided by the state) and management of budget difference (the state provides only part of the funds).

Total budget management

The budgets of the cultural units that adopt this method may cover all the funds needed or funds needed only for one or several items. Cultural units that adopt this form of management submit their plans and the basis on which these plans were drawn up, for verification and approval by the higher departments. Units that use this type of budget are mainly government cultural organizations and cultural establishments such as libraries, cultural halls, art galleries, and literary and art research academies (institutes). This is because they have practically no income of their own and rely mainly on state appropriations to cover the expenses for their activities.

Budget difference management

Cultural units that adopt this form of budget need help from the state to cover only a part of the funds for their professional activities. They submit a report on their budgets, together with the basis on which they are drawn up. Then the higher departments verify their incomes and expenditures and decide on the amount of subsidy to give these units. Any surplus after the accounts are balanced is placed at the disposal of the departments concerned. Units that adopt this form of budget are mostly performing-arts troupes and cultural departments having a certain amount of income from their activities. These departments can use part of such income to cover their expenditures.

After introducing this method, the state worked out regulations for the use of the year-end surplus funds of the cultural establishments concerned. According to these rules, any surplus of special funds must be used for special activities, while the remaining funds are used mainly to improve working conditions and promote various cultural undertakings. They cannot be used to raise the staff members' wages, wilfully increase the expenditures or extend their scope. Bearing in mind the interests of the state and the collective, the departments concerned may use part of the funds derived from increased revenue and reduced expenditure for collective welfare and also for awards to individuals in accordance with the proportion agreed upon between these departments and their higher departments.

The above-mentioned method, which is still being tried out, has yielded fruitful results and played a positive role in arousing the enthusiasm of cultural departments and in letting their staff members manage financial affairs as masters of their country, improve financial management and the use of funds, and extend the sources of income and reduce expenditure.

PLANS FOR CULTURAL DEVELOPMENT

Since the adoption of the method mentioned above, the state allocates funds on the basis of the central and local plans for the development of cultural undertakings. These plans consist of long-term (ten years), medium-term (five years) and annual plans. In drafting the plans, the goal in developing various cultural undertakings is defined, the scale, targets and key items of cultural development are determined, and the guiding principles and chief measures for fulfilling the plans are formulated. On this basis, the budget targets and the tasks for the departments concerned are decided. The programmes for the cultural undertakings are drawn up by the governments and government cultural-management organizations at various levels on the basis of investigation and study. The governing principle is the following: on the basis of the state's actual financial, material and human resources, to effect a comprehensive balance, to develop the various cultural undertakings in a planned and proportionate way, and to work hard to meet gradually the many-sided needs of the people in cultural life, promote the flourishing and development of culture and art, and encourage socialist ethics and thought.

STATE ASSISTANCE TO LITERARY AND ARTISTIC CREATION

The state guarantees the wages, housing, medical treatment, place of work and funds for the vocational activities of writers, artists and other cultural workers. Old people who can no longer work also enjoy state pensions, subsidies, medical care, housing and other forms of welfare assistance. Concern is also shown for folk artists' work, and proper arrangements are made for their material well-being.

There are now 839,000 professional cultural and artistic workers, of whom 442,000 are under the Ministry of Culture. The government encourages writers and artists to study theory, devote themselves to their work, enter deep into the realities of life and constantly raise their ideological consciousness and professional skills. Particular attention is paid to discovering and training young literary and artistic talents. Honours, material awards or bonuses are given for creative works and to individuals and organizations that have achieved remarkable results. The state also gives support and practical assistance to amateur writers and artists in their creative activities and accords honour, material awards or bonuses to those who have achieved outstanding successes. Government publishing and distributing departments print and distribute textbooks, academic, literary and art works, and journals of all kinds. Special arrangements are made for publishing the creative works of writers and artists. There are now 437 literary and art periodicals published and distributed at prefectural level and above. (See Table 3.) Remuneration is given for all articles printed. National and local theatres, auditoriums and recreation centres provide every facility for films and the performing arts. The state also allocates funds to various cultural undertakings to facilitate the smooth development of cultural activities. Ninety per cent of the nation's 3,483 professional performing-arts troupes received state subsidies in 1981, which accounted for 60 per cent of their total outlay. In addition, in order to promote the development of culture and art, the state earmarks in its budget special allocations for national and local theatrical and music festivals of various kinds and for making contributions, organizing competitions, deciding on awards and other forms of cultural activity.

The party and government show great concern and respect for writers, artists and other cultural workers. Many of those with remarkable achievements in creative and cultural work are elected as deputies to the people's congresses at various levels and as members of the Chinese People's Political Consultative Conference and they are held in high esteem by the people.

e building of a rural cultural centre
the Jingzhaofeng Commune of Shazhou
nty in Jiangsu Province has improved
cultural life of the people there.
e picture shows the commune members
ding newspapers and magazines.

the award ceremony for the best
ldren's books on 26 May 1982
Beijing, prizes were given to sixty-four
ters, editors and representatives
publishing houses.

The traditional dragon boat race held by
peasants in Nanhai county of Guangdong
Province on the fifth day of the fifth
lunar month to commemorate the death
of the poet Qu Yuan, who died more
than 2,000 years ago.

o Jinrong, vice-president
he Arts Academy in Gansu Province
Chairman of the Chinese
ncers' Association, has made bold
empts and achieved inspiring success
leveloping the Dunhuang school
ance. The picture shows Gao teaching
dents this style of dance.

Terracotta warriors and
horses excavated in
the No. 1 vault to the east
of the tomb of
Emperor Qin Shi Huang
(259–210 B.C.).

The art of paper cut-outs in Fushan County of Shanxi Province has a history dating back 1,300 years. Each of the 170 production teams in the county has experts, which has won it the title of 'Land of Paper-Cuts'. Wang Jiuming and his family are making cut-outs of flowers and animals for window decoration.

A huge collection of porcelain of the Yuan Dynasty (1279–1368) was excavated in the county town of Gaoan, Jiangxi Province. The picture shows some of the famous Jingdezhen porcelain that was discovered.

A bronze cart and warriors unearthed in Wuwei, Gansu Province.

Cultural policies:
practice and results

At present China's cultural undertakings are in a period of renewal and prosperity. The Chinese people, who value what they have won, will never forget the events of the recent past. From the summer of 1966 to the autumn of 1976, China underwent a decade-long Cultural Revolution that wreaked havoc on its cultural undertakings as a result of sabotage by the Lin Biao and Jiang Qing counter-revolutionary cliques. Taking advantage of the portion of party and state power they had usurped, these two cliques seized control of the leading cultural policy-making organs, used despicable means arbitrarily to distort, change and discard China's socialist cultural policies and enforce their reactionary cultural autocratic rule. They totally negated the cultural accomplishments achieved under the guidance of socialist cultural policies in the seventeen years since the founding of the People's Republic, ruthlessly attacked and persecuted literary and artistic workers, banned the splendid Chinese and foreign cultures, both ancient and modern, and dissolved most of the performing-arts units and cultural institutions.

There have been twists and turns in China's development, but the wheels of history never move backwards. The Chinese people finally won the victory in the struggle against these two cliques—a struggle that was vital to the country's future. In the winter of 1978 the Third Plenary Session of the Eleventh Party Central Committee decided to shift the focus of the task of the party and state to socialist modernization, an action that meets the aspirations of the entire people. Since then, China has embarked on a new stage of development.

In this new period of its history, the primary task of China's cultural undertakings is to set right the socialist cultural policies, revive their original features, make readjustments, and develop them to suit the changing reality of Chinese society. In this respect party and government departments and cultural policy-making organizations at all levels have done much effective work, thereby creating favourable conditions for the consolidation and development of China's socialist culture in line with socialist principles and policies.

The Fourth Congress of Chinese Literary and Art Workers, held from 30 October to 16 November 1979 in Beijing, was a meeting of historic significance, demonstrating that China's culture and art had embarked on a new road. (The Third Congress of Literary and Art Workers was held in 1960.) The central task of the Fourth Congress was to sum up the experience gained in literary and artistic work since the founding of the People's Republic in 1949, reaffirm socialist cultural principles and policies and define the tasks of literature and art in the new historical period. The congress was a success; it achieved the desired results and effectively rallied the literary and artistic workers throughout China to work jointly for the development and prosperity of socialist literature and art and for the building up of socialist ethics and thought.

The beginning of the 1980s saw China's various cultural undertakings continuing their advance under the guidance of the general policy of serving the people and socialism. An excellent situation prevails on the cultural front, and a new chapter in the history of China's cultural development has opened.

In retrospect, the new China's culture has in the past thirty-four years been through a resplendent spring and a harsh winter and has experienced its golden age as well as a period of dearth and depression. What accounts for all this? Our experience has shown that the gains or losses, successes or failures, the scale of achievements and the speed of development, as well as the degree of prosperity of China's culture and art, are all closely linked with the correct or incorrect implementation of cultural principles and policies. Very often they are in direct ratio with these. Gladdened by the present prosperous situation of China's cultural and artistic work, this writer cannot help but come to the conclusion that the main reason why China's cultural undertakings have taken on a new look and achieved so much in only a few years after suffering serious destruction is the effective implementation of socialist cultural policies.

Two points are worth noting when we consider the relationship between the cultural policies and cultural prosperity. First, although the practice of cultural policy and literary and artistic creation are related ideologically, they are two different concepts. This is because cultural policies cannot be equated with the methods of literary and artistic creation. Each literary or artistic form has its own specific method of expression. Even the revolutionary realistic method of creation advocated and used by our writers and artists can be applied in various ways, since writers and artists have different artistic styles. Cultural policies therefore demonstrate their power by propelling and promoting the prosperity and development of literature and art, but they cannot and will never replace literary and artistic creations themselves. Cultural policies do not restrict the freedom of creative activities, as has been explained in the chapter on China's cultural policies and principles. The policy of 'letting a hundred flowers blossom and a hundred schools of thought contend' requires that organizations in charge of implementing cultural policies should not interfere in the freedom of creation, but should promote and support this freedom.

Secondly, cultural policies are not aesthetic criteria for evaluating specific literary and artistic works; a work of art that conforms to the cultural policies in terms of ideology is not necessarily an excellent one. However, it cannot be denied that in China the correct and effective implementation of such policies is an indispensable condition and a guarantee for the creation of successful literature and art.

This being the case, this section of the monograph does not aim to prove the results of the cultural policies through the evaluation of particular works. Rather, it intends to discuss how fruitful results in culture and art have been achieved through the implementation of these policies. This corresponds better with the main idea we wish to expound. The following sections contain some of the main points.

Implementation of cultural policies ensures the development and prosperity of socialist literature and art

Effective measures have been adopted to put into practice socialist cultural policies and to do away with the mental shackles hampering literary and artistic creation. This has liberated the productive forces of literature and art. In literary and artistic creation the biggest obstacle was the theory of 'all-round dictatorship' concocted by Lin Biao and the Gang of Four over culture and art in the socialist historical period. Theoretically, the so-called 'all-round dictatorship' is utterly absurd. Proceeding from subjective idealism, Lin Biao and the Gang of Four alleged that there was a revisionist 'sinister literary and art line', and they branded the cultural policies, administrative organs, leading cadres of the literary and art departments and the broad masses of literary and art workers, who had opinions that differed from theirs, as the products of this 'sinister line' and imposed an 'all-round dictatorship' over them. After the downfall of the Gang of Four, struggles took place in order to eliminate the pernicious influence of the ultra-left line and reactionary policies. Measures taken in regard to the cultural policies fall into three categories.

First, with the powerful support of the Chinese Communist Party, the cultural-policy administrative departments, relying on the people and the literary and art workers, have vigorously propagated and carried out the socialist cultural principles and policies and promoted artistic democracy. In line with these policies, government cultural organizations have taken concrete action to rehabilitate the cultural organs and units, the literary and art workers, and the literature and art that had been attacked or persecuted by the ultra-left line and the reactionary policies of the Gang of Four. This move has been very encouraging and has won acclaim from the people, who are wholly in favour of the socialist cultural policies. Not only were the various obstacles in the way of the cultural cause removed but the broad masses of literary and art workers have liberated their minds and their enthusiasm for building a socialist culture has been greatly enhanced. Such enthusiasm found a quick reflection in their literary and artistic creation, and thus favourable conditions have been created for the flourishing of culture and art in the new historical period. China's theatrical arts are an example. Less than two years after the implementation of the correct cultural policies, more than 200 types of opera have been revived, over 2,000 theatrical troupes founded and more than 100,000 traditional plays restaged. All this has done much to bring about the rejuvenation of China's ancient theatrical arts.

Secondly, at the suggestion of the Chinese Communist Party and in line with the modernization drive in the new historical period, the government has summed up positive and negative experiences in literature and art since the founding of the new China and made important changes in the country's cultural policies. With regard to literary and artistic theory, the principle that literature and art should not be divorced from politics is upheld, but the proposition that 'literature and art should be subordinated to politics' has been changed. Moreover, the slogan 'literature and art must serve politics' is replaced by 'literature and art must serve the people and socialism', which is the general orientation and policy of cultural work in the new period. This has effectively prevented using simple administrative orders to interfere crudely in literary and artistic creation, and thus political guarantees are provided for the correct implementation of the cultural policies.

Thirdly, during the work to readjust cultural policies, the Chinese Dramatists' Association, the Chinese Writers' Association and the Chinese Film Workers' Association jointly held a forum on the writing of plays and film-scripts in February 1980, following the convocation of the Fourth Congress of Literary and Art Workers. They studied the new situation and the problems that had emerged in literary and artistic work. Party and state leader Hu Yaobang and others attended the forum. He joined in the discussions and made an important speech. The forum discussed the new problems encountered in the implementation of the cultural policies and categorically opposed the influence of the ultra-left line in literature and art. The forum reaffirmed the importance of the 'two-hundred' policy and discussed some important problems concerning literary and artistic creation and theories in combination with analyses of some controversial works. Questions discussed included the problems of truthfulness, tendentiousness and representativeness of literary and artistic works and social responsibilities of writers and artists, as well as the social effect of their works. The forum, which was permeated with an atmosphere of free discussion, played an important role and exerted a far-reaching influence on literary and art workers, helped them to understand and reflect the new era correctly, and promoted the flourishing of literature and art in the new historical period.

Awards to encourage literary
and artistic work

The administrative organs of the state for cultural policy sponsor contests and make awards at regular national or local theatrical, music and drama festivals, exhibitions, and through article or essay competitions. Such activities, which have state financial support, help promote the prosperity of literature and art. They clearly show the government's concern for cultural and artistic undertakings and demonstrate the superiority of the Chinese socialist system.

These activities, which help to enforce the socialist cultural policies, are carried out in a lively and effective way. Outstanding works are selected by professional literary and art workers from a large number of entries under the auspices of the cultural administrative organs at various levels. Representing the ideology and art of different regions, these works are rich and colourful in their choice of topic, style and form. The festivals, exhibitions and contests are attended by representatives from different places who democratically comment on the programmes and exhibits and exchange their experiences. Good artistic experiences are published in the newspapers or other publications, and works of art, individuals and units that receive awards are publicized in order to commend talent and encourage those who lag behind. To give the people of various regions a chance to enjoy and comment on the programmes and works that have won awards, the cultural administrative departments organize public and touring performances. These activities are carried out regularly and have gradually become a custom. They help not only to raise steadily the artistic level of professional literary and art workers but also to enhance the people's level of artistic appreciation. In this sense, these activities are a lively reflection of China's cultural principle of 'combining popularization with elevation'.

Over the last few years, guided by the 'two-hundred' policy, numerous awards of different kinds have been made in the fields of literature, drama, films, music, dancing, the fine arts, photography, calligraphy and television. In Beijing, the capital, such activities take place throughout the year. In 1980 twenty national award activities were made. The National Fine Arts Exhibition, which marked the thirtieth anniversary of the founding of the new China and was sponsored by the Ministry of Culture and the Chinese Artists' Association, honoured *People and the Premier* and eighty-one other works. A national song poll was sponsored by the Central People's Broadcasting Station, the Chinese Musicians' Association and the editorial department of the magazine *Songs* and *Toasting Song* and fourteen other lyrical songs received awards. A ballad-singing festival of amateur worker-artists and a theatrical festival of amateur peasant-artists, sponsored by the Ministry of Culture in co-operation with the departments concerned, rewarded forty-five items of the first category and thirty-three of the latter. The Second National Competition of Children's Literary and

Art Creations which lasted over a year and was sponsored by the Ministry of Culture, the Central Committee of the Communist Youth League, the China Federation of Literary and Art Circles, the Chinese Scientific Society and the Chinese Writers' Association, rewarded 212 pieces (44 with first prizes), 13 senior writers and artists who had excelled themselves in making contributions to children's literature, and 5 theatrical troupes. The First National Dance Contest, sponsored by the Ministry of Culture and the departments concerned, presented 206 newly created solo dances, *pas de deux* and trio performances; 46 people received awards for the best directing, 72 for the best performances, and 26 for the best music compositions, with *Fish Chasing* (a *pas de deux*), *Battle Drum at Jingshan* (a trio performance) and *Water* (a solo dance) taking the top honours. The National Calligraphy Contest, sponsored by the Shanghai magazine *Calligraphy*, received over 15,000 entries (including some from people of Taiwan origin, from residents of Hong Kong and Macao, and from Chinese now residing in America), with the eldest contributor aged 98 and the youngest 19 (middle- and primary-school students and professional calligraphers did not take part). Ten people won first prizes, twenty were awarded second prizes, and thirty third prizes and forty were honoured for their excellent work. In addition, awards were made for television shows, including those for children, held under the auspices of the Ministry of Radio and Television. China's film and literary circles have similar annual activities.

The biggest of the above-mentioned events was the National Theatrical Festival, which marked the thirtieth anniversary of the founding of the People's Republic of China and was sponsored by the Ministry of Culture. With a rich and colourful repertoire, the festival was held in Beijing and lasted for thirteen months, from 5 January 1979 to 9 February 1980. Of the 137 productions staged, 90 per cent were new works. The festival's complete cycle of programmes was given 18 times, with a total of 1,428 performances attended by 1.84 million people. Some excellent plays were performed to capacity audiences throughout. The festival gave a tremendous stimulus to literary and art circles. Its productions included sixty-one modern dramas, thirty traditional operas, twelve operas, two musicals, seven dance-dramas, three ballad-singing performances, two acrobatic shows, eighteen song and dance performances, and a puppet show. A hundred and twenty-seven theatrical troupes from twenty-nine provinces, municipalities, autonomous regions and departments under the State Council participated in the festival. Invitations were also sent to Taiwan Province.

During the festival, for the purpose of exchanging experiences, the sponsors held over 130 forums and invited experts, literary and art theoretical research workers and representatives of the general public to attend discussions on the festival's programmes, in the spirit of 'letting a hundred schools of thought contend'. The opinions were collected and published. A printed form was circulated among the festival participants, literary and art scientific research institutions and related departments for the purpose of obtaining opinions and support from all quarters. On the basis of this extensive opinion-soliciting, the festival's committee in charge finally decided on the items to receive awards and held a prize-giving ceremony on 8 April 1980, during which the names of the winners were announced. Two hundred and thirty-one items received awards for excellent creation or performance, sixteen of which took the first prizes for both. They were the modern dramas *Chen Yi Comes Down from the Mountains*, *Loyal Hearts*, *Dawn*, *Wang Zhaojun*, *Newspaper Boy*, *Song of the Storm* and *Spring Flower*; the Beijing operas *The Red Lantern Society* and *Chuncao Charges into the Court*; the Qin opera of Shaanxi Province *The Xian Incident*; the Henan Yu opera *County Magistrate Tang Tries Madame of Imperial Mandate*; the Guizhou Qian opera *Madame Shexiang*; the dance-drama *Silk Road*; and the operas *Venus*, *The Unjust Trial of Dou Eh* and the *Grand Marriage Ceremony*. The festival and the awards vividly demonstrated the achievements of the effective implementation of socialist cultural policies.

The development of literary criticism and the promotion of culture and art

In China the party and state leadership in culture and art is mainly reflected in the implementation of socialist cultural policies. To develop literary criticism in an energetic way is an important aid to carrying out these policies correctly. A serious attitude towards literary criticism is the result of summing up positive and negative historical experiences since the founding of the new China. As mentioned above, cultural policies themselves cannot be regarded as the aesthetic criteria for the evaluation of the quality of a particular work of literature or art, and of course they cannot replace literary criticism. Our country's cultural-policy administrative departments have asked that efforts should be made to develop literary criticism because of its significance in the implementation of cultural policies. They consider this an important measure that will influence literary and artistic creation and promote the prosperity of literature and art under the guidance of socialist cultural policies. The implementation of cultural policies is at the same time positive and tendentious, and particularly in the following two aspects.

The first aspect concerns the past. Because the implementation of socialist cultural policies was influenced by 'left' ideology and dogmatism, the departments for the administration of cultural affairs in certain places sometimes overlooked the fact that creation of works of literature and art is a complex mental process, and they neglected the basic laws of art. They therefore adopted inappropriate administrative orders and imposed over-simplified rulings on creative activities. This kind of action inevitably hampered the development and prosperity of literature and art and impaired the prestige of the cultural policies.

The second aspect concerns the present. In China today, because the influence of a number of ideologies left over from the old society is still in existence, the ideological struggle has not ended and various types of immoral behaviour, law-breaking, acts that violate discipline, and criminal activities of all kinds still occur. In the new historical period of socialist modernization, the task of socialist literature and art and the social responsibility of the literary and art workers have become all the more important and glorious. To build up socialist ethics, the cultural undertakings must adhere to the policy of serving the people and socialism. Hence, unhealthy tendencies manifested in literature and art should not be allowed to go unchecked. How can this be achieved in the implementation of cultural policies without at the same time interfering in a crude manner and letting erroneous tendencies develop unchecked? Practice over the past few years has proved that to strengthen literary criticism is an effective, scientific method. For instance, although the departments for the administration of cultural affairs do not interfere with the way in which writers and artists undertake their creative work, they may help them to understand the nature of society and reality amidst the complicated phenomena of social life and also help them to keep to the correct orientation of creation and to achieve success. Since literary criticism itself is carried out in the light of the policy of 'letting a hundred schools of thought contend', it encourages everyone to air their views and take part in discussions; it allows both criticism and counter-criticism, and helps to distinguish the truthful, good and beautiful from the sham, evil and ugly. It recommends the attitude of holding to the truth and correcting mistakes. This is a reliable way to pool collective wisdom and examine the social effect of literary and artistic creation.

In line with socialist cultural policies, to seek truth from facts is the principle that should be upheld in literary criticism. It calls for criticism of erroneous works, or of works with erroneous tendencies. However, this kind of criticism must be based on facts and should convince people by reasoning through artistic analysis. Oversimplified and exaggerated criticism is not allowed. At the same time, enthusiastic help should be given to good or comparatively good works, and excellent works should be given awards. This is because, in socialist China's literature and art, good and comparatively good works account for the majority and occupy the dominant position, while the number of unhealthy and bad works is small. In literary criticism vulgar, unprincipled praise and factionalism should be opposed.

In recent years, encouraged by the government, literary criticism has flourished as never before. Through seminars and forums of various kinds, the cultural-policy administrative organs, literary and art units and academic research institutions discuss and contend over questions of different literary and artistic phenomena, new artistic schools of thought and academic views. Various kinds of literary and art publications have been resumed. All this has provided favourable conditions for the development of literary criticism. China now has twenty-five kinds of publications devoted to literary criticism and literary studies and aesthetic theory. These include *Literary Gazette, Literary Criticism* and *Literary and Art Studies,* all being influential publications in the country. In addition, most of the 180 literary publications in the various provinces, municipalities, autonomous regions and at the central level run special columns for literary criticism and academic discussions. Government leadership in literary and art work has been effectively improved and strengthened thanks to such literary criticism, and the tremendous role of the cultural policies has been brought into play in promoting the development and prosperity of China's cultural and artistic undertakings.

The practice of strengthening criticism while carrying out the cultural policies fully demonstrates China's socialist democracy, and it can therefore be called a work method that promotes literature and art with socialist means. This method, which conforms to the law of development of socialist culture and art, has also promoted reforms in the method of management of culture. Since 1979 China has reformed its system of examining film-making, the performing arts and dramas to be staged. Take film-production for example. Before the examination system was reformed, whenever a studio planned to make a feature film or a documentary it could not start formal shooting until the script had been examined and approved by the film-management bureau under the Ministry of Culture. This method was well intentioned. The measure was meant to avoid economic and political losses by poor-quality films which would be unsuitable for circulation, although large sums of money had gone into their production. However, experience showed that this kind of good intention seldom paid, because tight controls had the drawback of restricting artistic creation. In fact, the film-management departments alone could never guarantee the quality of films. After the reform of the system of examining film-production, the right to produce films was transferred to the individual studios. This has not only greatly mobilized the enthusiasm of each film studio for production but has also enhanced the film-workers' sense of responsibility. In order to increase constantly the quality and quantity of films, they are making great efforts to raise their artistic level and are also receiving practical help from extensive film criticism. Admittedly, since film-production rights went to the film studios there has been a tendency on the part of some studios to go after quantity and they have produced a number of poor films. But here criticism will serve as a major means to change the situation fundamentally. After the reform of the system for examining film-production the purpose of socialist film management to produce more and better films was met. Take the quantity of feature films and stage documents, for example. Prior to the reform, the total number was fourteen in 1977 and forty-six in 1978. After the reform, the number rose to sixty-five in 1979 and eighty-two in 1980. The total number of films produced in the two years after the reform was 2.45 times that of the two years prior to the reform. The year 1981 saw a further increase, with the total number rising to 105 films and the quality of the films has also improved. Of course, these successes should not be attributed to the reform of the system alone. They are a result of the implementation of China's cultural policies, which have provided the cultural-management departments with the conditions whereby they can concentrate on making thorough investigations and helping the art-production departments solve practical problems. As a result, the relations between senior and junior departments have become more harmonious and co-ordinated, and work efficiency and achievements have increased markedly.

The struggle to discover and save the cultural heritage

During the ten chaotic years of the Cultural Revolution, China's national cultural heritage was destroyed to a serious extent. To create and develop the new socialist culture, it is necessary to struggle to discover and save the cultural heritage. The state has paid special attention to this. It has not only allocated large sums in support but has offered material guarantees. Guided by the principles of 'making the past serve the present' and 'weeding through the old to bring forth the new', government cultural departments have adopted various efficient measures to enable the rich cultural heritage to shine with added splendour.

RESCUING THE CULTURAL HERITAGE

China is utilizing modern science and technology to record the artistic skills and techniques of veteran artists, including folk artists, so that they can be passed on to the younger generation. Many of these artists with a high level of artistic attainment are now advanced in age. If we do not take timely measures, their valuable accomplishments will be lost for ever. In view of this, the Ministry of Culture is co-operating with the departments concerned in tape-recording and video-taping their singing and other performances. The China Art Research Institute sent special groups to Henan, Shanxi, Hebei, Sichuan, Shaanxi, Hunan and Tianjin to record and video more than 200 theatrical items of some 300 actors and actresses. Among them are such famous performers as Chen Jinbiao of the *puxian* opera, Ke Xianxi of the *gaojia* opera, Chang Xiangyu of the *yuju* opera and Gao Shenglin, Guan Sushuang and Li Huiliang of the Beijing opera. The Shanghai Art Research Institute has tape-recorded and video-taped more than fifty theatrical pieces by some seventy actors and actresses as well as the performances of various schools of *kunqu* opera during the productions marking the sixtieth anniversary of the famous *kunqu* artist Yu Zhenfei's stage career.

UNEARTHING AND COLLATING
THE CULTURAL HERITAGE

Only a small part of China's tremendous national cultural heritage is in written form, while most of it is handed down orally; Chinese operas and folk art and literature, for instance, are mainly retained in the memory of the artists. What is more, the work of digging up the cultural heritage was forced to stop for a decade during the Cultural Revolution. The government has therefore asked the cultural administrative organs at various levels and all quarters concerned to strengthen the work of discovering and collating. Remarkable successes have been achieved in the past few years. Professor Wang Yinuan of China's Northwest Institute of Minority Nationalities has devoted his efforts to unearthing the cultural heritage of the minority nationalities for some decades, and he has translated and studied *King Gesar*, an epic poem of the Tibetan people. In view of the various versions he has come across, he assumes that the entire epic may run to sixty volumes, with a million lines. This is rare in the history of world culture. Since the founding of the People's Republic, the departments concerned have concentrated on compiling this Tibetan epic. By the time the Cultural Revolution started in 1966, dozens of handwritten versions and valuable data had already been collected. Unfortunately most of these were burnt during the tumultuous years that followed. Now, however, a team co-sponsored by government cultural departments and the China Society for the Study of Folk Literature and Art has organized experts and those working on folk art in Tibet, Qinghai, Gansu, Sichuan and Yunnan to continue collecting, studying and translating this work. Good results have been obtained. Based on the material collected, a troupe in Qinghai created the opera *Expedition*, an episode from the life of King Gesar, as its contribution to the thirtieth anniversary of the founding of the People's Republic.

Another example is the *Manas*, an epic of the Khalkhas, which was compiled from the singing of several hundred folk singers in the area where this minority people live in compact communities. Most of it, however, was also lost during the Cultural Revolution. Luckily, the singer who performed in *Manas* is still alive. He has a good memory and can sing more than 200,000 lines of this epic poem. Now he is in Beijing, and a special group has been assigned to take down and edit what he sings. The opera will regain its lustre before long.

Yet another example is a special group for the study of the folk literature of the Manchu people, which was sent by the Cultural Bureau of Liaoning Province to Dandong to collect the legends, local customs and traditions, folk-stories and ballads of this people. It has already collected material totalling more than 50,000 words.

In addition, there are many organizations all over the country which are discovering and compiling China's rich heritage in the fields of literature, music, painting, drama and the applied arts.

INHERITING THE CULTURAL LEGACY

The aim in unearthing the cultural heritage is to 'make the past serve the present'. However, for a part of this heritage, the work cannot be accomplished by using modern science and technology alone. The performing arts, for example, can be inherited and carried forward only through the personal coaching of veteran artists.

Chinese drama is an example. It has more than 300 different local operas. To enable this ancient art to blossom, government cultural departments have made arrangements for the restaging of outstanding traditional works, and newly edited historical versions of various local operas. This has greatly advanced the work of restoring and developing Chinese drama. Traditional artistic experience and skills will shine with renewed splendour, and provide valuable examples for the creation of drama with modern themes, through the restaging of *Empty City Plot, Story of the White Snake* and *Women Generals of the Yang Family* (Beijing operas), *Jade Hairpin* and *Liang Sanbo and Zhu Yingtai* (Shaoxing operas), *Butterfly Lovers* (Sichuan opera), *Unexpected Encounters* and *Fifteen Strings of Cash* (*kunqu* operas), *Orphan of the Zhao Family* (*qinqiang* opera) and *Woman Judge* (*huaiju* opera). To facilitate the restoration and development of different artistic schools, Beijing dramatic circles have set up a group for the study of Cheng Yanqiu's art and invited Professor Zhao Rongchen to teach the Cheng school of Beijing opera—for example, *Queen He Rebukes Before the Emperor* and *Creek of Fenghe River*. Another group for studying Yan Jupeng's art has been set up, and the Yan school artists Yan Shaopeng and Zhang Shaolou have been invited to teach representative pieces of the Yan school of Beijing opera, such as *Zhuge Liang Goes to Offer His Condolences* and *Evacuating From Xuzhou*. Shanghai theatrical circles have set up special groups for studying Zhou Xinfeng's and Gai Jiaotian's schools of art, and have staged representative works. These activities have played a positive role in training actors and actresses in developing the various schools of art.

Fresh progress has been made in discovering China's heritage in literature, the performing arts, the plastic arts and horticulture. This can be seen from many new items performed on the stage in recent years. Tinged strongly with the characteristics of the minority nationalities and giving the audiences refreshing entertainment, they include the Manchu nationality's dance *Surging to the Sky*, the Deng people's dance *Morning Glory*, the Xiarba people's dance *Spring of the Xiarbas* and the Hezhe nationality's dance *Moving Straw Bundles*. Tibetan opera, *Baiju* opera and *Daiju* opera with their unique styles were seldom performed before and are now staged.

The famous Song Dynasty porcelain *jianzhan* teacups are a treasure of ceramic art. They were shipped to Japan and Europe in ancient times. However, the art of making such porcelain was lost for several hundred years. In recent years, more than a hundred *jianzhan* teacups have been made in the ancient style. Production of this famous porcelain will soon be resumed.

The peasant paintings from Jinshan County, near Shanghai, are another example. Most of the artists are middle-aged peasant women well versed in embroidery or weaving. Inheriting the traditional skills of folk art, they use brush and paper, instead of needle and cloth, to express in painting their feelings and their experience of life. When their pictures were exhibited at the International Fair in Brussels in September 1980 they were warmly acclaimed as works of the 'Eastern Henri Matisse'.

In socialist China the work of discovering the legacies of national culture is not something temporary. It is an important part of the implementation of cultural policies and also an important component in building up the country's culture. It will grow and improve in the wake of the development of various cultural undertakings.

Making use of intellectual resources and training competent personnel

To ensure the continuing development of culture, the government has expanded art education in a planned way for various types of professional personnel, in addition to giving in-service training, especially to young and middle-aged people whom they have discovered. In the past, there were no schools specializing in training *quyi*—comic-dialogue, story-telling and ballad-singing artists. Later, some art schools opened *quyi* courses that could meet only part of the need. Although there are drama schools to train performing artists or other related professionals, they still fall short of the objective needs. Therefore, those artistic troupes that have the possibility are encouraged to run 'troupe schools' or restore the traditional way of passing on the technique (i.e. apprenticeship) and to train actors, actresses, directors, musicians and stage designers. In the fields of literature and film-making, apart from restoring various training courses, attention is paid to those young people who have shown promise, to help them gain experience, improve their artistic accomplishment and mature rapidly.

Boldness in assigning work is needed if we are to discover and develop competent personnel through in-service training. There are not enough film writers, directors, actors, actresses, photographers and designers. The talents of young and middle-aged graduates from art schools have not been given full play, and they are slow in reaching artistic maturity, owing to a lack of experience. As film production has developed rapidly in the past few years, the gap between objective needs and the limited number of artists available is quite wide, both qualitatively and quantitatively. However, the situation has improved since the principle of boldness in assigning work was put into action. Quite often a film was either jointly directed by veteran and young directors, or the 'new hand' was the managing director and the 'old hand' acted as the adviser. This has enabled young directors to acquire the ability to work independently. Among the eighty-two feature films and film versions of stage performances produced in 1980 thirty were shot with young people as directors. Besides, many new stars have already distinguished themselves on the screen.

Making awards to excellent creative works also helps the growth of young writers. Most of the literature that has been rewarded in recent years is that of young or middle-aged writers, many of them budding talents on the literary scene. Among those whose medium-length novels or short stories have been rewarded, well over half are young and formerly unknown authors.

Group after group of outstanding artists and writers has come to the fore as a result of the efforts made in recent years to discover and train new talent. They have already become a sizeable force in China's cultural and artistic undertakings. The danger of not having enough competent young people to take over our cause does not exist.

China's developing
cultural undertakings

Friedrich Engels, one of the founders of Marxist theory, made a comprehensive and profound study of the culture of mankind. He thought that for a great nation there was no catastrophe that could not be compensated for by historical development. The progress of Chinese history has borne out the correctness of his words. After the catastrophe of the Cultural Revolution, the Chinese entered a new historical period, and their various cultural undertakings have added to their record fresh achievements which carry forward the fine traditions of their culture and have written a new chapter in its history. These achievements, of course, have been won in the present-day reality of China after arduous efforts and struggle. In the present state of development, they still have some shortcomings and defects and fall far short of the demands of the Chinese people. Moreover, as they advance, the Chinese people are bound to meet with numerous new problems and they still have to overcome many difficulties. China's cultural undertakings in the new period, too, will continue to advance and develop on a rugged path, but they will go on to make new contributions to the cultural progress of mankind.

Literature

China's literary scene in the new period presents a very lively picture, and literary creativity is blooming now that the socialist cultural policies have swept away the various obstacles in the way of advance. Poetry, prose and reporting are in the forefront, and veteran and young writers vie with each other in their creative efforts. Their enthusiasm for expressing their feelings in the form of poetry, in particular, has not waned. More than 30,000 poems in various styles were published in the literary journals in the various provinces and municipalities in 1980. The achievements in the novel and the short story are also notable, and reflect the contemporary scene. According to a rough calculation, more than 3,000 short stories were published in literary journals in the provinces and municipalities throughout the country, and heartening results have been obtained in the search for fresh themes and ways of artistic presentation.

The writing of medium-length novels has also increased. Eighty-two were published in 1979, and in 1980 the number jumped to 172. This increase in number is something unmatched since the founding of the People's Republic in 1949; the range of themes and the achievements in depicting the new period and new people are also heartening.

More than ninety full-length novels were published in 1980—the best crop since the founding of the new China. It is significant that the ideas guiding the writing of such novels have gradually matured, and some fine works that successfully depict the true features of history and the characteristics of the new period have appeared.

The major characteristics of literary creation in the new historical period can be listed. With respect to the ideas guiding literary creation, the style of revolutionary realism has been restored and developed while the fine traditions of Chinese literature have been carried forward and new breakthroughs have been made in ideological depth to reflect the reality in China today. As regards themes, as the various restrictions upon literary creation have been removed and one-sidedness in literary theory has been overcome, the sphere for reflecting life has been broadened, and since literature is now more closely linked with reality it can better portray the characteristics of the times. In artistic presentation, bold experiments have been made to create new material. Many writers, especially the middle-aged and the young, have courageously broken new ground by drawing upon China's traditional literary experiences and on those of other countries to create varied forms, styles and artistic skills.

In recent years China's cultural administrative organizations have on several occasions sponsored the selection of outstanding literary works. Those selected reflect in a measure the new achievements and the heights to which literary creation has attained in the past few years.

To date, four national selections of outstanding short stories (from 1978 to 1981) have been sponsored by the editorial department of *Renmin Wenxue* (People's Literature) and the Chinese Writers' Association. Readers in all fields of work throughout the country took an active part in recommending their choices. More than a million recommendation letters were received. Giving due consideration to these recommendations and the appraisals of specialists, 100 fine short stories were selected in those four years. In both 1978 and 1979 twenty-five works were awarded prizes. Among them were *The Head Teacher of a Class, Director Qiao Assumes Office* and *A General in a Small Town*, all of which were welcomed by the people. Thirty short stories were selected in 1980. Among those most liked by the readers were *Anecdotes From the Western Front*, by Xu Huaizhong; *In a Village*, by He Shiguang; *Lunar Eclipse*, by Li Guowen; *The Stupid Old Wang*, by Jin Yun and Wang Yi; *Diaries of a Factory Secretary*, by Jiang

56

Zilong; *Chen Huansheng Going to the City*, by Gao Xiaosheng; *An Empty Nest*, by Bing Xin; *The Melodies of Spring*, by Wang Meng; *A Love-Forsaken Corner*, by Zhang Xuan; and *The Story of a Living Buddha*, by Mala Qinhu.

As a result of the selection of outstanding short stories produced in 1981 twenty works received awards, including Wang Runzi's *My Wife*, Zhao Benfu's *Selling a Donkey*, Wureertu's *The Entreaties of a Hunter*, Chen Jiangong's *The Flower Scarf Has Floated Away*, Zhang Yigong's *The Black Boy Has a Picture Taken*, and Liu Shaotang's *Mount Emei*—all with a strong flavour of life and written in diverse styles. The writing of short stories in the past two years has kept abreast of the times, vividly depicting the new features of the period, the growth of a socialist new people, and the road ahead.

In the national selections of fine medium-length novels written in the period 1977–80, outstanding reports produced in the same period, and distinguished new poems by middle-aged and young poets, which were activities sponsored by the Chinese Writers' Association, prizes were given to eighty fine works. Of these, fifteen were for medium-length novels, thirty for reporting, and thirty-five for new poems.

Of the fifteen medium-length novels, five won first-class awards and ten won second-class awards. (See Table 4.) The five works that won first-class awards were: *When One Reaches Middle Age*, by Shen Rong; *On a River With No Navigation Marks*, by Ye Weilin; *The Legend of Tianyun Mountain*, by Lu Yanzhou; *The Story of Prisoner Li Tongzhong*, by Zhang Yigong; and *Butterfly*, by Wang Meng.

All these prize-winning works have portrayed in depth the joys and sorrows as well as the wishes and demands of the people, vividly depicted their lofty thoughts and truthfully recorded their march forward in the socialist modernization drive of the new period.

Here we wish also to mention the satisfactory developments made in the past few years in children's literature and popular science literature, both of which developed very slowly in the past. The Chinese Writers' Association has set up a children's literature group, a children's literature society and a society for the study of children's literature and art as well as other mass academic organizations. All are working hard now to enrich the cultural life of the more than 300 million Chinese adolescents and children. In 1979 more than 800 books and journals for children were published, a 100-per-cent increase over 1978 and a fourfold increase over 1977. Apart from the fact that many journals of literature and art have opened special columns for publishing works for children, literary and art journals specially catering to children increased to 28 in 1980. With the continuing popularization of scientific and technical knowledge, people working in the fields of science, literature and art have paid greater attention to popular science literature. In 1979 the science columns of newspapers throughout the country published more than a thousand pieces of science fiction, short scientific essays and fairy tales. Some good works were awarded prizes.

TABLE 4. Prize-winning medium-length novels produced from 1977 to 1980

Title	Author	Published in	Class of award
When One Reaches Middle Age	Shen Rong	Shouhuo (Harvest)	1st
On a River With No Navigation Marks	Ye Weilin	Furong (Lotus)	1st
The Legend of Tianyun Mountain	Lu Yanzhou	Qingming, No. 1, 1979	1st
The Story of Prisoner Li Tongzhong	Zhang Yigong	Shouhuo, No. 1, 1980	1st
Butterfly	Wang Meng	Shiyue, No. 4, October 1980	1st
Soil	Wang Zhecheng, Wen Xiaoyu	Shouhuo, No. 6, 1980	2nd
PLA Women Who Went after Their Units	Deng Youmei	Shiyue, No. 1, 1979	2nd
Ah!	Feng Jicai	Shouhuo, No. 6, 1979	2nd
Red Yulan Magnolia under the Wall	Cong Weixi	Shouhuo, No. 2, 1979	2nd
Families by the Catkin Willow	Liu Shaotang	Shiyue, No. 3, 1980	2nd
The Light Morning Fog	Zhang Kangkang	Shouhuo, No. 6, 1980	2nd
Forerunners	Jiang Zilong	Shiyue, No. 6, 1980	2nd
A Three-Generation Stone	Zong Pu	Shiyue, No. 3, 1980	2nd
Sweet Gooseberry	Sun Jiangong	Furong, No. 1, 1980	2nd
A Soul-Stirring Act	Lu Yao	Dangdai (Contemporary Era), No. 3, 1980	2nd

With the flourishing of literary creation in recent years, the number of writers has also expanded continuously. Now the Chinese Writers' Association has a total of 1,550 members, of whom 223 are new members, accepted in recent years. Of these new members, 70 per cent are middle-aged and young writers. At the same time, local branches of the Association in all parts of the country keep in contact with an additional 700 young writers under the age of 35. All this shows that middle-aged and young writers have become a new force in China's literary creation.

International literary exchanges have also increased in recent years, friendly contacts with foreign writers have been established and interflow has increased. From 1979 to 1981 China sent a total of 134 writers, literary critics and translators to fourteen countries and regions for visits. At the same time the Chinese Writers' Association played host to 130 writers from ten countries and regions of the world. In order to expand the exchanges between Chinese writers and literary circles in other countries and promote the progress and prosperity of literature in the world as a whole, the China Pen Centre was founded in April 1980, and it joined the International P.E.N. in May of that year. Later, the Shanghai Pen Centre and Guangzhou Pen Centre were founded. They were accepted as members by the International P.E.N. in February 1982.

At present, Chinese literary circles are summing up experiences and are determined to achieve more, overcome shortcomings and create closer links to work for the prosperity of literature.

Art

The scope, level and orientation of the development of various forms of art are yardsticks in judging China's aesthetic achievements.

By the end of 1981 China had 3,483 performing-arts units of various kinds, including modern-drama theatres, art theatres, opera theatres (or companies), dance-opera troupes, philharmonic orchestras, chorus groups, cultural ensembles, drama troupes (or companies), *quyi* troupes (including ballad-singing, story-telling, comic dialogue, clapper talk, cross talk, etc.), acrobatic troupes, circuses, puppet-show troupes, shadow-show troupes; 602 of them belong to the national minority autonomous areas. In addition, China has 450 organizations for art creation, 2,599 performing centres, 26 art exhibition centres and 64 art research institutions. (See Table 5.)

Drama, *quyi* and acrobatics, which have time-honoured traditions, are closely linked with the people's life. However, in politically decadent old China they were on the verge of extinction. Since the founding of the new China, these folk arts, which are popular in various parts of the country, have, with the energetic support of the People's Government, developed gradually until today there are 2,612 professional performing troupes. About 60 per cent of them are state owned and about 40 per cent collectively owned. After entering the new period of construction, taking the principle of letting a hundred flowers blossom, weeding through the old to bring forth the new and making foreign things serve China, the nation has adopted the policy of simultaneously developing traditional dramas, dramas with historical themes and dramas with modern themes. In practice, different types of drama and troupes are encouraged to develop their own styles and strong points. The result is that a flourishing and heartening situation has emerged. Some items in the traditional repertoire that are still considered good are restaged, and at the same time a number of new dramas with modern themes have been created, such as the Shaanxi opera *The Xian Incident*, the Shaoxing opera *Song of the Newspaper Boy*, the Beijing opera *Nantian Zhu*, the Han opera *Mouldy Money*, the *Liuqin* opera *Xiaoyan and Dayan*, the farce *An Excellent Answer*, the Shanghai opera *The Disdained*, the Huai opera *The Judgment of Love*, the *Gezi* opera *Spring of the Double Swords*, the flower-drum opera *Sanliwan*, the Yunnan opera *Song of Welcome to the Spring* and the *Pingju* opera *The Trumpeter Sues*. All these operas reflect from different angles the Chinese revolutions of different historical periods and have won encouragement and acclaim from audiences across the country.

Quyi is a form of art the Chinese people like very much. It successfully uses speech and song to reflect the people's thoughts and feelings. For instance, the *meihua dagu A Bowlful of Milk*, the clapper talk *Marshal Peng Dehuai Growing Wheat*, the story-telling in the Beijing-dialect *Mount Meiling* and the *pingshu An Excellent Move in Chess Play*—all give a vivid account of the heart-stirring deeds of the late Zhou Enlai (Chou en Lai), Peng Dehuai and Chen Yi whose memories are deeply cherished by the Chinese people. The comic dialogue *Talking False, Big and Empty*, by using artistic language, portrays a political swindler who is clever at telling lies, talking 'big and empty' and speaking nonsense. These are some of the forms used to criticize the poisonous influence of the ultra-left ideology. The *pingtan*, in Suzhou dialect, *A New Pipa*[1] and *Who Is the Most Beautiful*; the *pinghua*, in Yangzhou dialect, *Inside and Outside the Window*; and the *zhuizi*, in Henan dialect, *The Sweet Girl* are all ideologically good and artistically superb works. In addition, the traditional *quyi* repertoire, after being revised, is once again resplendent. *The Story of Yue Fei*, a *pingshu*, has been broadcast by sixty radio stations in the country, apart from being performed in some story-telling centres and theatres, thus becoming a popular item which people enjoy listening to after meals or during their spare time. In order to promote the development of *quyi*, which has a total number of 168 performing troupes throughout the country, the cultural departments have sponsored special *quyi* festivals and prize-giving activities and done much work in training *quyi* artists.

China has 113 acrobatic troupes and circuses. Techniques have attained new heights, and new items have been added in recent years. For instance,

1. A guitar-like four-stringed instrument.

the item *Juggling a Person with the Feet While Balancing on a Springboard*, performed by the Shanghai Acrobatic Troupe, combines the movements of juggling and balancing in an intricate and harmonious way and is therefore a feat of originality and unique artistic perfection. *Rolling Cups*, performed by teenagers of the Guangzhou Acrobatic Troupe, has incorporated the techniques of modern callisthenics with acrobatics and is particularly lively and graceful. With regard to the circus, the giant panda is playing a wonderful role. Panda Wei Wei of the Shanghai Acrobatic Troupe has learnt how to juggle a bucket and perform other tricks to the delight of the audiences, thereby adding new lustre to the circus.

Music, dance, opera and modern drama are newly emerging arts in China. Most troupes specializing in these arts have grown out of former cultural ensembles and performing-arts teams set up during the war years. The philharmonic societies, orchestras for traditional Chinese music, ballet troupes, national dance-drama troupes and opera theatres were all established in the mid-1950s after the new China was founded. Now there are 871 such performing-arts units in China, including 37 song-and-dance troupes, 9 opera troupes, 8 opera theatres (or companies), 4 ballet troupes, 8 philharmonic societies, 3 orchestras of traditional Chinese music, a chorus, 2 broadcasting art troupes and 82 modern-drama troupes (or companies). They are all fairly big and have an influential effect on society. Their artistic achievements are in many respects representative of the country's standards.

Modern Chinese drama has restored and carried forward the revolutionary realistic tradition and now is vigorously marching forward, keeping pace with the socialist modernization drive. In recent years a number of works have appeared that reflect the actual life in China today, and embody the spirit of the era. For instance, *Royal Hearts*, which won an award in the art festival celebrating the thirtieth anniversary of the founding of the new China, and *Flowers Heralding the Spring* are typically good works. As China moved into the 1980s, playwrights and artists put the stress on creating images of revolutionary heroes and socialist new men who are typical of the spirit of the new era. This is a characteristic of the modern dramas. Works such as *Mayor Chen Yi, Blood Is Always Hot, Neighbours, Who Is the Strongest* and *Love of the Motherland*, while being scathing satires on the ugly phenomena of present-day life, also sing the praises of the good things in society and the lofty ideals of the people. These works are achievements in seeking new artistic methods of expression.

In order to advance the Chinese performing arts, we have, in accordance with our cultural policies, continued to stress the importance of drawing upon and developing our fine artistic traditions in creating and fostering socialist music and dance; in addition to this, we learn from the art of other countries which has become part of the world's heritage, introduce famous foreign writers and their works to the people and use foreign artistic forms to reflect our country's past and present life and make

61

them a component part of our own music and dance. To this end, we have structurally separated the performing units for traditional Chinese music and dance from those for foreign music and dance. For example, we have established the Central Philharmonic Society of Traditional Chinese Music, the China Opera and Dance Theatre, the National Song and Dance Ensemble as well as opera and dance troupes at provincial, municipal and autonomous regional level, which all specialize in traditional Chinese art forms. Apart from these, we have established the Central Philharmonic Society (which includes a symphony orchestra and a chorus), the Central Opera Theatre and the China Ballet Company, which specialize in foreign art forms.

China's national dance-drama has made remarkable progress in recent years. For instance, the full-length dance-dramas *On the Silk Road, Princess Wen Cheng* and *Zhaoshutun and Nanmu Ruona* are new successes in this field. *On the Silk Road,* which has dance movements based on the murals and statues of the famous Tunhuang Grottoes, a historic beauty spot, is a unique and exquisite dance-drama portraying the economic and cultural exchanges and friendship of the Chinese people at the height of the Tang Dynasty with the people of neighbouring countries. It is reminiscent of the old Silk Road of that time, and it has won warm acclaim from the Chinese people and from China's friends the world over.

Worth noting also is the government's concern for and interest in the foreign art form of the symphony. Since its establishment, the orchestra of the Central Philharmonic Society has regularly held concerts to introduce to the Chinese people the symphonic works of various schools in foreign countries as well as the symphonic works of Chinese musicians. In 1980 alone this symphony orchestra played seventy symphonies, of which sixty-five were foreign and five were Chinese. In May 1981, the Ministry of Culture and the Chinese Musicians' Association co-sponsored the first national poll for symphonic works, and twenty-four provinces, munici-palities and units of the People's Liberation Army submitted, after initial selection, ninety-six symphonic works. The result was that thirty-five works won awards. Six were given 'outstanding' awards, twelve 'fine' awards and seventeen 'encouragement' awards. It can be expected that China's level of symphonic music will steadily improve.

China's drama, music, dance and acrobatics occupy an important position in its cultural exchanges with other countries. In 1980, it sent thirty-two delegations and groups to visit fifty-eight countries and regions. It also sent delegations to the international piano competition in Montreal, the international Chopin piano competition, and the international ballet competition in Japan, thus making positive contributions to promoting friendship between the Chinese people and those of other countries.

Painting has also achieved success in recent years. Traditional Chinese painting, oil painting, engraving, caricature, picture-story books, New Year pictures and other styles have developed rapidly. The flourishing of the

TABLE 5. China's art organizations

Organizations	Total	State-owned	Collectively owned
Creative	450	449	1
Performing			
Modern drama troupes, drama troupes for children, farce troupes	104	90	14
Opera troupes, dance troupes, song and dance troupes	152	141	11
Song and dance troupes of national minorities	34	33	1
Symphony orchestras and choruses	10	10	
Cultural troupes, literary and art propaganda teams	529	472	57
Ulan Muqi (mobile troupes on the pastureland)	76	76	
Opera theatres	2 272	1 254	1 018
Beijing opera theatres	221	137	84
Quyi troupes	168	46	122
Acrobatic troupes and circuses	113	59	54
Puppet shows	47	16	31
Shadow shows	12	1	11
Centres	2 599	2 262	337
Research	64	64	
Exhibition	36	36	
Other	84	60	24

fine arts has made it possible to hold numerous exhibitions in various parts of the country. During the 1979 Spring Festival alone, 20 exhibitions of paintings were held in Beijing; in 1980 about 400 exhibitions of paintings were held throughout the country and about 10,000 fine works were displayed. Exhibitions were also organized for such famous painters as Lin Fengmian, Liu Haisu, Huang Xinbo, Yu Ben, Qian Songyan, Huang Yongyu, Wu Guanzhong as well as the late He Xiangning, Fu Baoshi and Situ Qiao. In addition, exhibitions of paintings by young and middle-aged painters of various schools were held. These exhibitions reflect the varied themes, forms and styles in the country and present the unprecedentedly thriving situation since the founding of the new China.

The traditional arts and crafts have also made much headway. Take for instance the ivory carving *Toast in Honour of the Bright Moon*, by the newly established Guangzhou Ivory Carving Arts and Crafts Factory. As big as the fist of a small child, the ivory ball has forty-five revolving layers, each carved with beautiful flowers. This ivory ball has the most layers of any of its kind ever made in China. The snuff bottle carved with the design of the Luoyang Xingdian Pavilion by the Glazed Art Products Factory in Shandong, the wood carving *A Dragon Boat* by the Shanghai

Arts and Crafts Carving Factory, and the big ivory carving *Ouxiang Pavilion* produced by the Beijing Ivory Carving Factory, by absorbing the techniques of ivory and jade carving of various schools, are all art treasures.

The development of the fine arts has brought forth a great number of new talents. By the end of 1981 the Chinese Artists' Association, which has a total membership of 15,000, had set up branch associations in all the provinces (except Taiwan), municipalities and autonomous regions. There are now over forty fine-arts magazines throughout the country.

With the development of the arts, works with unhealthy ideological and artistic contents and meaning have also appeared. The art workers are aware of this phenomenon and are striving to overcome it and to raise the quality of the arts through evaluation of experiences and literary criticism.

Films

In the new period of construction, China's achievements in revitalizing and developing its film industry are encouraging. Before the Cultural Revolution started in 1966, China had laid quite a solid foundation for film production, having thirteen studios, of which seven produced feature films, one animated films, one newsreel and documentary films, three scientific and educational films and one dubbed foreign films in Chinese. In the last few years, apart from enlarging and reinforcing the former thirteen studios, China has built five new studios to produce feature films, of which three were built in areas where the national minorities live in compact communities, the purpose being to strengthen cultural development there. Now China has altogether eighteen studios, twelve of which are feature-film studios that can produce about a hundred feature films and film versions of stage performances a year.

Films enjoy a huge market in China. In fact, it is the largest market, attracting an ever-growing public. In the seventeen years from the founding of the new China until the beginning of the Cultural Revolution in 1966, China produced 603 feature films and film versions of stage performances, and in the five years after the Cultural Revolution, it produced 300. Although the film industry has developed at a relatively rapid rate, it still cannot satisfy the growing needs of the broad masses of the people. This shows that there are great prospects for the development of this industry in our country.

In recent years, the artistic level of Chinese films, including ideological contents, subject-matter and style, has seen a new breakthrough and development. To encourage and commend the Chinese film-workers for their achievements in the new historical period, the Ministry of Culture conferred the Fine Film Award on the best films produced in 1979, 1980 and 1981. The Chinese Film Workers' Association sponsored the third, fourth and fifth Hundred Flowers Award polls in 1980, 1981 and 1982.

(The first and second polls were held in 1962 and 1963.) In 1981, the Chinese Film Workers' Association initiated the Chinese Film Gold Rooster Award. Films that have won such awards in these years include the features *Tear Stain*, *Little Flower*, *Evening Rain*, *From Slave to General*, *Inside and Outside the Court*, *Look at This Family*, *Anxious to Return*, *Romance on Lushan Mountain*, *Legend of the Tianyun Mountain*, *The Young Teacher*, *The Nanchang Uprising*, *In-Law*, *Neighbours*, *Call of the Home Village* and *A Love-Forsaken Corner*; film versions of the stage performances *A Minor Official* and *Story of the White Snake*; the cartoon and puppet films *Three Monks* and *Nezha Conquers the Dragon King*; the newsreel and documentary films *Song of the Pioneers* and *Lushan Mountain*; and the scientific and educational films *Life and Protein: Synthetic Insulin* and *The Kingdom of Bees*. All these films have been well received by the people as well as by experts. (See Tables 6, 7 and 8.)

With many new writers having come to the fore, the number of scenarists has expanded rapidly in recent years. The thriving situation in script-writing has brought with it active film criticism. Research on cinematographic theories has received due attention and has been augmented. The Chinese Film Workers' Association publishes four national film magazines: *Cinematographic Art*, *World Cinema*, *Cinematographic Techniques* and *Popular Cinema* (which sells 8 million copies a month). In addition, its branch associations and film distribution units in the provinces and municipalities publish magazines of various kinds on films that, needless to say, have a wide influence and a great appeal to the people in China.

In order to enable the people living in both the cities and countryside to see films, the state, while energetically promoting the production of films, has made great efforts to increase the number of projection units. By the end of 1981, China had altogether 130,000 film-projection units, of which 30 per cent work in the cities and 70 per cent in the countryside. However, because the country has a big population and the economy is not very advanced yet, 35-mm projectors are used in only about 16 per cent of the cinemas throughout the country. In the countryside, because of the shortage of cinemas, films are mostly shown in the open at night and the projectors are mainly of the 16-mm and 8.75-mm types. In recent years the government has taken measures to raise the quality of film projection. In addition to new cinemas built in a planned way, 2,600 government auditoriums and clubs have been made available for showing films. In the rural market towns the state has built more than 1,800 cinemas and simply equipped film-projection halls, with the result that the conditions for film-showing have improved in both urban and rural areas.

China follows a policy of low-price tickets and charges for films. In the areas where the national minorities live in compact communities, films are subsidized or exempt from all charges in order to make them available to people living in the countryside, mountain areas, frontier regions and on the islands.

TABLE 6. Winners of the Fine Film Award conferred by the Ministry of Culture

	Films produced in 1979	Films produced in 1980	Films produced in 1981
Feature films[1]	From Slave to General (two parts) Tear Stain General Ji Hongchang Anxious to Return Ah Cradle A Troubled Laughter Little Flower Shots in the C.I.B. Reverberations of Life Flowering Cherry Aolei Yilan (two parts) Day Dawn A Heart in Sorrow A Loyal Overseas Chinese Family The Moon Over a Fountain Li Siguang Guide Look at This Family Bus No. 3 Two Sets of Twins A Sacred Mission North Star	Evening Rain Legend of the Tianyun Mountain Inside and Outside the Court A Young Hero The Tenth Bullet Hole Unmelted Snow The Young Teacher The Man Who Deals With Devils	In-Law Neighbours The Xian Incident The Nanchang Uprising The Drive to Win A Long Way to Go Regret for the Past Call of the Home Village A Love-Forsaken Corner A Green Wallet (a feature film for children)
Film versions of stage performances	Romance of the Iron Bow	Story of the White Snake	Li Huiniang
Animated films	Nezha Conquers the Dragon King Avanti Mimi The Lazy Kitten	Three Monks Snow Boy	Dr Nan Guo

1. Documentary films, scientific and educational films and dubbed films that won the award are not included.

66

TABLE 7.   Winners of the Hundred Flowers Award

	Third poll for films produced in 1979	Fourth poll for films produced in 1980	Fifth poll for films produced in 1981
Features	*General Ji Hongchang* *Tear Stain* *Little Flower*	*Romance on Lushan Mountain* *Legend of the Tianyun Mountain*	*In-Law* *Call of the Home Village*
Films of stage performances	*Romance of the Iron Bow*	*A Minor Official*	*Story of the White Snake*
Animated films	*Nezha Conquers the Dragon King* *Avanti*		
Scenarist	Chen Lide for the film *General Ji Hongchang*		
Director	Xie Tian for the film *Planned Parenthood: A Joyous Cause*		
Actor	Li Rentang as Zhu Keshi in *Tear Stain*	Da Shichang as Lin Hanhua in *Come Home Swallow*	Wang Xingong as Cai E in *Intimate Friends*
Actress	Chen Chong as Zhao Xiaohua in *Little Flower*	Zhang Yu as Zhou Jun in *Romance on Lushan Mountain*	Li Xiuming as Xu Xiuyun in *Xu Mao and His Daughters*
Supporting role	Liu Xiaoqing as Zhang Lan in *Look at This Family*		
Photography	Chen Guoliang and Yun Wenyao for *Little Flower*		
Music	Wang Ming for *Little Flower*		
Art designer	Huang Qiagui for *They Have a Family*		
Documentaries	*Eternal Glory to Respected and Beloved Zhou Enlai* (Chou en Lai) *Melody of Beauty*		
Scientific and educational films	*Yellow Weasel* *Under the Traffic Lights*		

67

TABLE 8.   Winners of the Gold Rooster Award

	First poll for films produced in 1980	Second poll for films produced in 1981
Honourable award		*In-Law*
Feature	*Evening Rain* *Legend of the Tianyun Mountain*	*Neighbours*
Documentary	*Eternal Glory to Comrade Liu Shaoqi*	*Song of the Pioneers* *Don't Idle Away Your Life*
Scientific and educational	*Life and Protein: Synthetic Insulin*	*Kingdom of the Bees*
Animated film	*Three Monks*	
Scenarist	Ye Nan for *Evening Rain*	Zhang Xian for *A Love-Forsaken Corner*
Director	Xie Jin for *Legend of the Tianyun Mountain*	Cheng Yin for *The Xian Incident*
Actor		Zhang Yan as Jiang Changfu in *Laughter in Moon Village*
Actress	Zhang Yu as Zhou Jun in *Romance on Lushan Mountain* Zhang Yu as Liu Wenying in *Evening Rain*	Li Xiuming as the fourth daughter in *Xu Mao and His Daughters*
Supporting actors	Shi Ling, Ouyang Ruqiu, Mao Weihui, Lin Bin, Zhong Xinghuo, Lu Qing won the collective award for the supporting roles in *Evening Rain*	Sun Feihu as Chiang Kaishek in *The Xian Incident*
Supporting actress		He Xiaoshu as Ling Hua in *A Love-Forsaken Corner*
Photography	Xu Qi for *Legend of the Tianyun Mountain*	Zhou Jixun for the films *Regret for the Past* and *Xu Mao and His Daughters*
Art designers	Ding Chen and Chen Shaomian for *Legend of the Tianyun Mountain*	Han Jixun, Qu Yanxin and Li Huazhong for *Midnight*
Music	Gao Tian for *Evening Rain*	Yang Shaolu for *In-Law*
Recording		Zhang Ruikun for *The Drive to Win*
Cutting and editing		Fu Zhengyi for the films *Regret for the Past* and *Intimate Friends*
Best special award		Ge Rongliang, Chen Jizhang and Zhou Haofei for the film version of the stage performance *Li Huiniang*
Costume		Cao Yingping for the films *The Nanchang Uprising* and *The Story of Ah Q*

68

TABLE 8 *(continued)*.

	First poll for films produced in 1980	Second poll for films produced in 1981
Make-up		Wang Xizhong and Li Ende for *The Xian Incident*
Properties		Liu Qingbiao for *Neighbours*
Special award	Xiang Juanzhu in the dubbed feature film for children *The Young Teacher*	Director Zhang Nuanxin in the newsreel and documentary film *The Great Wall of Iron and Steel* and the feature film *The Drive to Win*

Today, more than 3,900 distribution and projection companies have been set up at central, provincial, municipal and autonomous regional levels as well as at the prefectural and county levels, and film-distribution stations have been set up at the commune level. These companies and stations are responsible for the management of all the cinemas, clubs and film-projection teams throughout the country as well as being in charge of delivering film copies to the projection units in both urban and rural areas.

The state has set up a national cinematographic equipment corporation to arrange for the production and supply of projection equipment, spare parts and accessories and to conduct the import and export of cinematographic equipment. In addition, there are 264 supply and repair centres for such equipment in the provinces, municipalities and autonomous regions across the country. In order to ensure efficiency in film distribution and film projection, China has set up fourteen cinematographic technical schools or training classes in the various provinces, municipalities and autonomous regions. In addition, the film distribution and projection corporations in some provinces, prefectures and counties run courses at irregular intervals to train their own projectionists and managers. China now has 440,000 people in charge of film distribution, projection, equipment supply, repair and management.

Along with the expansion of cultural exchanges with foreign countries, China has established film import-export business connections with sixty-three countries and regions of the world. In 1979 it set up a joint film-making corporation to produce films in collaboration with other countries and to offer labour or to provide assistance to other countries on the basis of friendship and mutual benefit.

The film industry has developed rapidly, and the film projectors produced in the country today are now more than adequate. Although colour negatives and diapositives are still of poor quality, China is self-sufficient as regards black-and-white positives, colour positives, and black-and-white negatives, all of which are in great demand. The film-processing industry has also made much progress. In addition to the two big film-processing factories in Beijing and Shanghai, all the film studios and some of the film factories have laboratories of their own. Altogether, China now has forty film-processing factories (or laboratories), doing all the work of processing copies.

The Ministry of Culture recently held a national conference on script-writing, at which achievements and experiences were discussed and summed up, new problems arising in this sphere were tackled, and the unhealthy tendencies that have appeared in some films were studied. At the conference, film-workers expressed their determination to make still greater efforts to improve the quality of socialist films by keeping abreast of the times and absorbing ideas from the people.

Popular cultural undertakings

China has a population of 1,000 million, of whom about 800 million are peasants. If the peasants were to be ignored when developing China's cultural undertakings, it would be an error of orientation and it would be meaningless to talk of achieving a high level of socialist culture; to show concern for the cultural life of the peasants is of major importance in developing mass-culture undertakings. With the development of agricultural production and the increase in collective economic strength in recent years, the material life of the peasants has been improved. This has provided favourable conditions for the development of cultural undertakings. In order to promote these undertakings, the government has adopted the principle of 'strengthening leadership, striving for active and steady development, proceeding from the actual conditions of various places, doing what is possible and devoting attention to achieving actual results'. Guided by this principle, cultural organizations under local governments at various levels and the departments concerned have worked in collaboration. Their concerted efforts have made the popular-culture undertakings progress at a steady pace. According to the latest statistics, China now has 2,893 cultural halls, 1,787 libraries, 28,417 commune-run cultural stations, 3,607 rural-town cultural centres, 1,856 rural-town cinemas and theatres, 90,645 rural film-projection teams and 78,013 opera troupes and spare-time performing organizations which mainly serve the countryside. In all, there is a backbone force of over a million people for rural cultural and artistic activities. At present, the situation of popular-culture work in the country is excellent and the scope and quality of activities are being steadily improved.

In recent years, the government has adopted the following major methods to promote the development of popular-culture undertakings.

ESTABLISHING CULTURAL CENTRES
IN RURAL TOWNS

Practice has proved that an effective way of encouraging a new socialist countryside is to transform the rural towns into the political, economic and cultural centres of their areas. Rural cultural centres are a new idea which conforms to the historical trend of the times and is in keeping with the aspirations of the peasants. They are popular-culture organizations that organize activities concerned with culture, art, education, popular science, sports and public health in the countryside. Usually they incorporate such basic units as cinemas, theatres, film-projection teams, opera troupes, libraries (reading rooms), recreation rooms (clubs), playgrounds, cultural stations, broadcasting stations and popular-science organizations. As the cultural centres are set up in rural towns that are frequented by the peasants, they do not have to go far to see a film or an opera and to read books. These cultural centres have played a positive role in satisfying the diversified cultural needs of the peasants.

Moreover, as they develop mainly by relying on the collective economic strength, and as they are closely linked with the interests of the peasants, they will prosper with the continuing progress of agricultural production. An example is the experience of Xinchang Town of Nanhui County in Shanghai. Xinchang Town has a population of 30,000, including both urban residents and peasants. With the development in the town and the surrounding villages, the peasants often come to the town to see films or operas, buy books or take part in popular-science activities or sports activities. In order to meet the needs of the peasants for cultural life, the town authorities have merged the cultural centre, club, sports committee and children's centre, as well as the cultural station, film-projection team and library belonging to the Xinchang People's Commune, into a single establishment. All the organizations co-operate to sponsor various popular cultural activities, with 3,000–4,000 people taking part every day. During holidays, the cultural activities are more colourful. The town's streets are neat and clean. Everything is in good order. A scene of prosperity meets the eye everywhere.

Another example is the Zhengji People's Commune in Tianchang County, Anhui Province. The commune has a population of more than 19,000. Zhengji, the commune site, is a remote rural town with some 1,000 people. In the past there was little cultural life to speak of. The people used to complain: 'We peasants have only three things to do every day—eat, work and sleep.' In order to change this situation, the commune pooled funds to build a simply equipped cinema theatre, a library, a photo studio and a television room. They also built an open basketball court and organized a spare-time opera troupe. The cultural centre staged seventy-one performances in a year for an audience of 55,000, and showed 568 films for an audience of 480,000. More than a hundred people visit the library every

71

day. The cultural centre also actively carries out scientific and technical activities. For instance, it has run training classes on agricultural science and technology and trained more than 500 activists for scientific farming. This small cultural centre earned 24,500 yuan in one year. After paying the wages of its staff members and the administrative expenses, it had a surplus of 9,000 yuan. This has prepared the material conditions for its own development.

In places where the cultural centres are well run, people spend their after-work hours in a proper and healthy manner, taking part in various recreational activities. Since superstitious activities and cases of gambling, theft and quarrels have been drastically reduced, social order has improved greatly. Facts have proved that running the rural cultural centres well plays a positive role in achieving a high level of socialist morality and ethics.

PAYING ATTENTION TO MASS CULTURAL ACTIVITIES DURING FESTIVALS

China is a multinational country. Apart from International Labour Day and National Day, which are celebrated in common by all nationalities, each nationality has its own traditional festivals, such as the Spring Festival of the Han nationality, the Water-Sprinkling Festival of the Dai people, the Torch Festival of the Yi people, the Dragon Boat Festival of the Miao people and the Tibetan New Year. The people of various nationalities all have the tradition of holding mass cultural activities during their festivals. Great attention is being paid by the government cultural departments to this. Usually various meetings are held every year to discuss and make plans for such activities during the festivals. The cultural centres and stations as well as popular-art centres are charged with the task of training amateur mass-culture activists and supplying singing and performing materials. Stage performances are also organized for the festivals. To get a better understanding of the mass-culture activities of the people of all nationalities in China, we shall here give as examples the Spring Festival and the Water-Sprinkling Festival.

The Spring Festival is a traditional day of celebration for most people in China. It is celebrated not only by the Han nationality, whose population constitutes the overwhelming majority throughout the country, but also by many minority nationalities. The way in which mass-culture activities are carried out during this festival is an important yardstick for determining whether popular-culture work is done well or not. According to reports from all parts of the country, mass-culture activities during the Spring Festival of 1980 were unprecedentedly colourful. In many places there were cases where father and son, mother and son, grandfather and grandson, brothers and sisters or sisters-in-law performed, sang or danced together. According to statistics from Guangdong Province, during the Spring Festival of 1980 more than 4,300 spare-time opera troupes in the rural areas staged performances, more than 210,000 people took part in performances, and mass-culture activities were held in 80 per cent of the province's production brigades. In recent years, all cultural centres or stations, palaces and rooms throughout the country have organized such cultural activities as singing, film and lantern-slide shows, and exhibitions to publicize among the people family planning, socialist democracy, the socialist legal system and scientific knowledge as well as commending the advanced units and individuals. Rich and colourful folk-culture activities, such as flower fairs, lantern festivals, lion dancing, dragon lanterns, *Yangge* dancing, walking on stilts, land-boat dances and bamboo horses, have been held both in the cities and in the countryside. Some age-old folk arts that had practically disappeared have been brought to life again during the Spring Festival. It is really a joyful occasion for the people. It fully demonstrates the stability and unity in the new historical period of China's socialist modernization.

The Water-Sprinkling Festival of the Dai people starts on 24 June of the Dai calendar (13 April of the Chinese lunar calendar) and lasts three days. On the first day, a grand dragon-boat race is held on the Lancang River and the people dance in the villages or in the fields. On the second day, the people sprinkle water on one another and wish one and all happiness and good luck in the coming year. With the old and young singing and dancing, it is really an attractive scene and a happy occasion. On the third day, the people go to the rural fairs to buy farm tools and daily necessities. As dusk falls, they dress in their festival best, sing and dance till dawn around bonfires and under colourful lanterns in the coconut forests. On 14 April (lunar calendar) 1961 the late Chinese Premier Zhou Enlai (Chou En Lai), dressed in Dai clothes, celebrated the Water-Sprinkling Festival together with the Dai people, and wished them happiness. The people were so happy that their eyes filled with tears of joy. They played their *Jinzhubi*, a wind instrument made of bamboo, and danced the *Xiangjaogu* (elephant's-leg drum) dance. Premier Zhou left a deep impression in the minds of the Dai people, for he respected the customs and habits of the minority peoples and shared their happiness.

GIVING THE CULTURAL CENTRES (STATIONS) THE MAIN ROLE IN POPULARIZING CULTURAL KNOWLEDGE AMONG THE MASSES

To set up cultural stations in the people's communes, cultural centres in the counties and popular art centres in the prefectures is an important method of strengthening mass-culture work, promoting mass-culture and mass-art activities, providing a richer cultural life for the people and raising their scientific and cultural level.

Cultural centres have been set up in all counties and city districts

73

(including those under the municipalities, which in turn are under the central authorities and cities which are under the provincial governments). They have two major tasks. One is to organize mass singing and performances and exhibitions as well as to run cultural classes and training classes in scientific and technical knowledge; they not only animate the cultural and recreational activities of the people, publicize the government's principles, policies, decrees and state laws, but also help raise the people's cultural and scientific level. The other task is to provide guidance for the people's leisure-time cultural and art activities and collate national and folk art. Major ways of providing guidance include training working personnel for the cultural stations and amateur cultural and art activists, supplying the people with singing and performing materials, setting up models and publicizing the experiences. Some cultural centres also organize rural cultural work teams, which go into the country to give performances or provide guidance for the masses, carry out investigations and collect folk art. This is an effective method and is appreciated by the people.

Cultural stations are the basic organizations for promoting mass-culture activities at grass-roots level, and 40 per cent of the rural people's communes have now set up such stations. Their task is, on the one hand, to organize the people in mass-culture activities such as singing and performing, reading, attending exhibitions, film and lantern-slide shows and, on the other, to provide guidance for spare-time mass-culture activities.

The country's twenty-nine provinces, municipalities and autonomous regions (except Taiwan) as well as the cities under the provincial governments have now established popular-art centres. Their major tasks are to guide and train cadres and mass-culture activists for the cultural centres at county and district levels, supply singing and performing materials, do organizational work for collecting folk literature and art and sum up and publicize experiences gained in mass-culture activities.

With the development of mass-culture work in recent years, satisfactory results have also been achieved in leisure-time literary creation in country areas. For instance, rural cultural activists in Jianyang County, Sichuan Province, have produced more than 10,000 literary and art works in the past three years, some of which have been staged in national theatrical festivals or displayed in exhibitions. Leisure-time rural literary creation not only includes poems and novels but also operas, screenplays, and musical and art works as well.

In addition, since various forms of production responsibility have been adopted in country regions, the peasants' demands for scientific knowledge to increase output have become more urgent. For this reason, the commune-run associations to popularize scientific knowledge have come into being. They have mobilized all technical personnel (professional technicians, 'peasant experts' and skilled and experienced people) in the commune to provide scientific and technical services under the guidance of the county science associations, sign technical contracts, hold technical exchanges, publicize scientific knowledge and run training courses. They have played an important role in promoting agricultural production. In many places where cultural centres have been set up, the popularization of scientific knowledge has now been listed as one of the tasks. This has been welcomed by the peasants.

Literature and art of the minority nationalities

Since China entered the new period of socialist modernization the literature and art of the minority nationalities have embarked on a fresh stage in their development.

First, the government pays great attention to exploring and saving the cultural legacies of the minority nationalities. Twenty-nine provinces, municipalities and autonomous regions have now set up institutes of folk literature. Their major task is to explore and collate the literary and artistic heritage of the minority nationalities, which is also a task for the cultural centres (stations) throughout the country. The Chinese Academy of Social Sciences has set up an Institute of Minority Literature, which has a branch in Yunnan Province in south-west China. Teachers of languages and literature in all institutes for nationalities and some universities have jointly formed a society for the study of the minority peoples' literature. Folk literature has been made a speciality in universities of arts.

In order to revive the cultural heritage of the minority nationalities, government cultural departments, institutions of folk literature and institutions of higher learning, guided by the principle of 'collecting all and collating key pieces and making efforts in popularization and research', have co-operated with each other and formed working groups to go to these areas to investigate, collect and record folk-songs and folk-dances. Their efforts have yielded notable results. For instance, eight volumes of the epic *Manasi* (a hero of the Kirgiz nationality) have been recorded and are now being collated for publication. Manuscripts and xylographic copies of the world-famous epic of *King Gesar* (Tibetan) have been assembled and more than ten volumes have been published in Tibetan, with a circulation of more than 300,000 copies.

In order to promote literary creation among the minority nationalities, the Chinese Writers' Association and the State Nationalities Affairs Commission jointly held a national conference on literary creation of the minority nationalities in July 1980. The conference summed up experiences in developing the minority peoples' literature and art, held discussions and drew up work plans. It has exerted a wide and profound influence on the development of this kind of literature and art.

Towards the end of 1981 the State Nationalities Affairs Commission and the Chinese Writers' Association again collaborated in sponsoring the first national selection of distinguished works of minority peoples' literature produced in recent years. As a result, 140 good novels, poems, prose articles, literary works for children, reportages and screenplays by 138 writers of 38 nationalities were selected and given awards. Of these, forty were written and published in the Mongolian, Tibetan, Uygur, Korean, Kazak, Dai, Lisu, Jingpo, Kirgiz and Xibe languages. Until then, Tibet had not produced a single full-length novel; but in 1980 and 1981 it produced three, two of which were selected and given awards. The Qiang, Blang, Jingpo and Drung peoples have all ended the backward systems of keeping records by cutting marks on a piece of wood or tying knots in a piece of string. They have now, for the first time in history, their own writers and literary works.

It is most noticeable that a generation of talented writers has matured among the minority peoples. According to incomplete statistics, more than a thousand of them have joined the Chinese Writers' Association and the Research Society of Chinese Folk Literature and Art as well as branches in all parts of the country. They have laid a solid foundation for the flourishing of the minority peoples' literature and art.

In recent years, in order to keep pace with and encourage the development of literary creation among the minority nationalities, various journals devoted to publishing their folk literature, art and works have appeared throughout the country, in addition to the re-publication of *Minjian Wenxue* (Folk Literature), a national magazine, and the publication of *Minzu Wenxue* (Literature of Minority Nationalities), the nation's first literary journal of its kind. Among the newly published journals are *Caoyuan* (Grassland) in Inner Mongolia, *Shancha* (Camellia) in Yunnan, *Nanfeng* (Customs and Habits in South China) in Guizhou, *Shanhaijing* (Journal of Geography) in Zhejiang, *Chufeng* (Hunan's Customs and Habits) in Hunan, *Yuefeng* (Guangdong's Customs and Habits) in Guangdong, as well as similar journals and publications in Jiangsu, Shanxi, Henan, Jilin, Heilongjiang, Gansu and Liaoning. The state publication departments also pay great attention to the publication and circulation of books of folk literature, science and technology as well as history of the minority nationalities. The Shanghai Literary and Art Publishing House has edited and published more than ten selections of folk-tales and folk-songs of various nationalities. *Outline of Folk Literature, The Cultural History of China's Minority Nationalities* and *A Selection of Literary Works of China's Minority Nationalities* were all compiled and published to meet the needs of teaching in the institutions of higher learning of the minority nationalities and in other universities.

Academic research on the folk literature and art of various nationalities is also in full swing. Last year the China Research Society of Folk Literature and Art and the Society of Minority People's Literature held their first annual meetings on separate occasions. In addition, symposiums were held in Gansu, Zhejiang, Liaoning and Yunnan. Apart from reading academic papers, these meetings and symposiums exchanged experiences gained in collecting and studying the folk cultural heritage and in literary creation of the minority nationalities. They will play a significant role in further promoting the development of the minority peoples' literature and art.

Art education

The new China's achievements in literature and art abundantly prove that it now has a contingent of writers and artists who can stand the storms of struggle and are deeply loved by the people. The rejuvenation and expansion of this contingent mainly depend on the fresh blood transfused into it by the continuing development of socialist educational undertakings. Since China entered the new period of socialist modernization greater importance has been attached to discovering and training talented people. Art education has been rapidly restored and developed. A new generation of talented artists with special training has appeared on the literary scene, adding lustre to the prospering socialist literature and art.

By the end of 1981, China had established twenty-seven art colleges (including twenty-one special colleges for film, drama, traditional opera, music, dance, the fine arts, and arts and crafts, plus six comprehensive art colleges) and seventy-nine secondary art schools, with a total enrolment of more than 18,000. In addition, forty-nine teachers' universities and colleges and one comprehensive university have art departments, which specialize in training music and art teachers for middle and primary schools. Cultural organizations at the prefectural, city and county levels often run art courses and train literary and art cadres for the grass-roots units. Spare-time art education is also a part of art education as a whole. Cultural departments and organizations in many provinces and municipalities have opened art-study groups, which play a significant role in publicizing literature and art and in discovering talented people for further training.

The government has shown particular concern for training artists from among the minority peoples. Prior to the founding of the new China, there was practically no art education for the minority nationalities. After the founding of the People's Republic, nine art colleges and schools were set up in areas inhabited by compact minority communities, such as the five autonomous regions of Inner Mongolia, Xinjiang, Tibet, Guangxi and Ningxia, as well as Yunnan and Qinghai and the Yanbian Korean Autonomous Prefecture in Jilin Province. At the same time, special branches of art were made available in the central and local institutes for nationalities. Special classes and teachers' classes for the minority nationalities were also opened in some well-established art universities and colleges. Since the founding of the new China, various kinds of art colleges and schools have trained more than 7,000 art-workers. Many of them have become famous stars and leaders in present-day art circles. For instance, the Tibetan Caidan Zhuoma, the Uygur Rebiya, and the Mongolian Meer Jiehu are all famous singers liked by the people. Wang Dui, formerly a Tibetan serf, now is the deputy head, director and actor of the modern-drama troupe of the Tibet Autonomous Region. He was also elected a council member of the Chinese Dramatists' Association. Of the more than fifty minority nationalities in China, over thirty now have their own cadres specialized in the arts, and they play an important role in developing literature and art in areas inhabited by the minority peoples and in inheriting and carrying forward the literature of the minority peoples.

China's art colleges and schools enrol the best of those who take the unified examinations. In addition to strict professional requirements, all students are required to have good-conduct marks and a certain level of cultural knowledge. While in school, those recruited are required to devote their major energy to the study of basic knowledge and skills so as to lay a good foundation for their future careers. At the same time, they study the history and theory of their specialities and political theory, as well as cultural knowledge necessary for their future work. Normally, the period of study for the various specialities in art colleges is four years. The period for music, dance and traditional opera in secondary art schools is six or seven years and for fine arts four years. Everyone who completes his studies and passes examinations is given a diploma and assigned work by the state.

All the art colleges and schools in China have the system of people's subsidies. In recent years, some colleges have experimented with the system of combining such subsidies with scholarships. At present, 75 per cent of the students in the art colleges get grants or scholarships, and all the students in the secondary art schools get subsidies. In addition, students of certain subjects that require good physical condition, such as opera, dancing and instrument playing, are given diet subsidies to ensure their good health.

The principle of 'making the past serve the present and making foreign things serve China' is implemented in art education. Various types of art colleges and schools are asked, in line with their professional demands, to provide active guidance to enable the students to inherit China's fine cultural traditions and experiences in a scientific manner, to study and learn from good foreign literature and art, to organize students to see foreign art exhibitions and performances held in China and listen to lectures by foreign experts.

In order to raise the students' professional level, particular attention has also been paid to arranging the curriculum. For instance, the institutes of fine arts have departments of Chinese painting and oil painting. The first lays stress on learning the traditional skills of Chinese painting while the latter pays more attention to the techniques of Western oil painting. While the China Conservatory of Music takes the teaching of Chinese traditional music as its major task, the Central Conservatory of Music lays emphasis on Western music. Both the Beijing College of Dancing and the Shanghai Municipal School of Dancing have departments of national dancing and ballet. This is conducive to training professional artists.

In art education attention is also paid to practice, which has been made an important link in teaching. Some stage performances produced in recent years, such as *Macbeth* by the Central Drama Institute and *The History of the Qing Imperial Court* by the Shanghai Drama Institute, as well as the Beijing opera *The Tale of the White Snake* by the China Opera Institute and the ballet *Swan Lake* by the Beijing Institute of Dancing, have achieved fairly good results and are much appreciated by the audiences. During the 1980 national selection of works in the fine arts by young artists, the two prize-winners, the oil painting *Father* and the series of woodcuts *Qiu Jin*, were created by students of institutes of the fine arts. In the past two years some students in music conservatories were selected and sent to international music competitions. All of them have made satisfactory progress. The stage performances and works of fine art mentioned above all show that China's art education is making steady progress.

Publishing

Paper and printing were invented in China, and book publication also has a long history in our country. They have played an important role in the preservation of the splendid ancient culture of the Chinese nation and contributed greatly to the progress of human civilization. However, during the long feudal period, publishing made slow progress. In modern times, China was reduced to the status of a semi-colonial and semi-feudal society. Compared with some developed capitalist countries, publishing has lagged. With the birth of the new China, it began to take on a fresh look and great opportunities have been opened up for its development.

Publishing in the new China is of a socialist nature. Since the founding of the People's Republic in 1949, it has developed with the development of the country's economic construction, and there have been tremendous achievements.

In the last part of the 1970s, when China entered a new stage of development, in order to make up for the serious losses brought about by the Cultural Revolution, the government publishing administrations, guided by the socialist cultural policies, adopted various measures to improve publishing. After years of consolidation, restoration and reconstruction, publishing, printing and distribution organizations have made much headway. An excellent situation now prevails in publishing houses. In 1981, 111 of them were national publishing houses and the rest of them were at provincial level. The total staff in these establishments was 18,000. At the end of 1981 there were 176 printing houses in the country (not including printing houses that mainly print newspapers and other matter). The total annual production capacity of books and periodicals had increased to thirty-one times that of the early period of the People's Republic, which only had a capacity of 670,000 reams of paper. In 1981, books totalling 5,578 million copies were put on sale, 163.5 per cent more than in 1965, the peak year before the Cultural Revolution, and 45.4 per cent more than in 1977. These figures indicate that China's publishing undertaking is in a new and flourishing stage of development.

There is a publishing administration bureau under the Ministry of Culture, and the various provinces, municipalities and autonomous regions have their own publishing bureaux. The Publishing Administration Bureau under the Ministry of Culture is in charge of the publishing plan for the whole country. It works out unified regulations for publication, co-ordinates and administers publication, printing, distribution and the supply of paper. This is all for the purpose of enriching the people's cultural life, raising the scientific and cultural level of the Chinese nation and promoting socialist ethics and intellectual civilization.

China's publishing undertaking implements the system of division of labour for publishing, printing and distribution, each managing its own specialized affairs. Under the unified leadership of the Publishing Administration Bureau, managerial organizations, each with its respective function and powers, have been set up. All the publishing establishments in China are funded with investments from the state, which provides the necessary material conditions and manpower. Books of various kinds are brought out by special publishing houses that are responsible for the publication of books of a certain category.

All books are sold and distributed by the Xinhua Book Store through a distribution network of 6,000 centres and about 60,000 book-selling stalls attached to the supply and marketing co-ops and commercial departments.

The Foreign Languages Publishing and Distribution Administration Bureau, under the Ministry of Culture, is in charge of publishing and distributing books in foreign languages. The Guoji Shudian (China Publications Centre), the China National Publishing Industry Trading Corporation and the China National Publications Import and Export Corporation are in charge of distributing Chinese publications abroad.

To popularize scientific and cultural knowledge rapidly and meet the

TABLE 9.   The increase in the publication of books in recent years

Year	Titles	Copies (unit: 10,000)	Annual growth rate (percentage)	
			Titles	Copies
1977	12 886	330 804	—	—
1978	14 987	377 424	16.2	14
1979	17 212	407 178	14.8	8
1980	21 621	459 298	25.6	12.5
1981	25 601	557 830	18.4	21.5

requirements of the four modernizations, a low-price policy for books has been implemented by the state. Thus the large quantities of paper needed for printing books and of newsprint (not including high-quality paper) are subsidized by the state. In addition, the publishing houses turning out books for minority nationalities, the Braille publishing houses and the foreign-languages press are subsidized by the state.

Over the past few years, steady progress has been made in book publication. (See Table 9.) In 1977, 12,886 titles with a total of 3,308 million copies were published. By 1981, the figure had increased to 25,601 titles with a total of 5,578 million copies, an increase of 98 per cent and 68.6 per cent respectively over 1977. Compared with 1971, the titles turned out in 1981 showed an increase of 228 per cent and the number of copies printed rose by 130 per cent.

As can be seen from Table 10 and Table 11, readers in 1981 could get a better understanding of the Chinese people's cultural requirements in the new era. In 1981, the titles and copies of art and literary books were 214 per cent more than those in 1977, or 9.7 times the figure for 1971. This rapid growth is a reflection of China's literary and artistic development and prosperity. The titles of books on the natural sciences and production techniques rose by 105 per cent over 1977, or 6.4 times the 1971 figure. The titles of books on culture and education increased by 755 per cent compared with 1977, or 32 times the 1971 figure. This is a reflection of the progress of China's modernization drive in the cultural field. The government has in

TABLE 10. Kinds of books published in 1981

Category	Titles		Copies (10,000)
	Total	Newly published	
General	18 776	15 338	283 086
Philosophy and social sciences	2 559	2 041	25 864
Culture and education	3 901	3 175	129 240
Literature and art	3 934	3 197	31 230
Natural science and technology	5 862	4 815	18 078
Juvenile and children's books	2 520	2 110	78 674
Textbooks	4 144	2 161	199 841
For universities and secondary technical schools	2 124	993	6 525
For middle and primary schools	1 184	562	183 497
For spare-time education and other needs	189	100	5 193
For teaching	647	506	4 626
Picture-books	2 681	2 355	74 903
TOTAL	25 601	19 854	557 830

TABLE 11.   Proportions between different kinds of general books
                            published in 1981

Year	Philosophy and social sciences	Literature and art	Science and technology	Culture and education
1971	1 847	404	911	121
1977	2 057	1 253	2 957	455
1980	2 091	3 322	5 715	2 095
1981	2 559	3 934	5 862	3 901
Increase over 1971 (%)	13.8	876.0	543.0	3 100.0
Increase over 1977 (%)	2.4	214.0	105.0	755.0
Increase over 1980 (%)	22.3	18.4	2.5	76.6

recent years shown great concern for children's culture, and this finds
expression in publications. Some 2,520 juvenile books with a total of
786 million copies (including picture-story books) were published in 1981,
accounting for 28 per cent of the total number of general books published
in the year, with the number of titles rising by 54 per cent over 1979.
In 1981, 4,144 titles with a total of 2,000 million copies of textbooks for
students of universities, secondary vocational schools, middle and primary
schools and spare-time schools were published, a 72.8-per-cent increase
over 1977 and 174 per cent more than in 1971.

Further stress is also being laid on the publication of books in the
languages of the minority nationalities. Twenty publishing houses for this
special purpose have been set up. In 1981, 1,904 titles with a total of
26.52 million copies in 18 languages of 14 minority nationalities were
published, including Mongolian, Tibetan, Uygur, Kazakh, Korean, Yi,
Kirgiz, Dai, Jingpo, Lisu, Lahu and other languages. At present, seven
provinces and autonomous regions have their own editing and translation
organs in charge of bringing out teaching materials in the languages of the
minority nationalities, and a fairly good foundation has been laid. The
Xinjiang Educational Publishing House, for example, has published over
700 titles of teaching materials in the Uygur, Kazakh, Mongolian, Kirgiz
and Xibe languages.

China's publication circles have attached great importance to bringing
out the kind of books which the people have been demanding for a long
time, which have an important bearing on the culture of the new period and
which can be completed only after years of effort.

China's first encyclopedia will cover fifty disciplines. The volume
Astronomy was published in 1980. It is planned that the *Chinese Medical
Encyclopedia* will consist of eighty-six volumes, of which the volume
Ear-Nose-Throat has already been published. An *Encyclopedia on Agri-
culture* is under compilation.

The new edition of the *Collected Works of Lu Xun*, with footnotes and explanations, has been brought out after years of work. The one-volume complete edition of *Ci Hai*, a comprehensive Chinese encyclopedic dictionary, and the first, second and third volumes of *Ci Yuan*, an encyclopedic dictionary of sources of words, which took several years to revise, have also been published. A *Lexicon of the Chinese Language* and a *Dictionary of the Chinese Language* are being compiled. The *Collection of Inscriptions on Bones*, in thirteen parts, whose chief editor was the late Guo Moruo, is being brought out. *The Year Book of the Chinese Encyclopedia, Year Book of Chinese History, Year Book of World Economy* and *Almanac of Chinese Publications* were brought out in 1980. In 1981 the *Almanac of Chinese Economy* and several other large works of reference were published. Many other kinds of reference books and materials for research workers have been published, one after the other.

The publication of academic works and treatises by well-known Chinese scholars has attracted wide attention. Xue Muqiao's *China's Socialist Economy* and *Some Questions of China's Economy at Present*, Xu Dixin's *On Socialist Production, Circulation and Distribution*, Zhu Guangqian's *History of Aesthetics in the West*, Qian Zhongshu's *Studies on Letters and Ideas*, Li Siguang's *An Introduction to Geomechanics*, Qian Xuesen's *Engineering Cybernetics*, Tang Aoqing's *Theoretical Method of Ligand* and Qian Weichang's *Variational Method and Analysis of Finite Elements* have aroused wide attention in academic circles both at home and abroad. Furthermore, foreign academic works and literary masterpieces translated into Chinese and published in China are on the increase, providing valuable references for Chinese academic workers and writers and artists.

The publication of Chinese periodicals has flourished in recent years as never before. In 1981 alone, there were 2,801 periodicals and magazines which had registered with the publication administrations, a 227-per-cent increase over the 856 in 1964. Among them, 1,582 were devoted to science and technology and they accounted for 56.5 per cent of the total. There are 437 literary and art periodicals, 288 devoted to the philosophical and social sciences, and 494 to other branches. (See Table 12.)

TABLE 12. Periodicals published in 1981

Category	Type	Copies (10,000)
Comprehensive	124	16 682
Philosophy and social sciences	288	23 391
Natural science and technology	1 582	23 281
Culture and education	259	20 918
Literature and art	437	43 595
Periodicals for children	44	16 001
Pictorial	67	3 313
TOTAL	2 801	147 181

The increase in the types of periodicals and in the number of copies printed reflects the demand for scientific and technological knowledge as well as the initiative taken by writers in various fields. However, some periodicals are poor in quality, and readjustments and improvements are needed.

Since the founding of the People's Republic, the Foreign Languages Press has published some ten thousand different books and picture-albums in twenty-four languages. As for periodicals, *China Pictorial* is now published in nineteen languages; *China Reconstructs*, a comprehensive monthly magazine, is published in English, French, German, Spanish, Arabic and Portuguese; *Beijing Review* is a weekly published in English, French, German, Spanish and Japanese; *People's China* is a monthly in Japanese; *Chinese Literature* is a monthly literary magazine published in English and French; and *El Popola Cinio* is a monthly in Esperanto. The publication of books in co-operation with other countries has also made headway in the last few years.

The publication of books is an important sector in the building of socialist ethics and an intellectual civilization in China. In view of the new situation and new problems and in order to improve further the quality of books and periodicals and set up normal procedures in publishing work, the state publishing administrations have in recent years revised the rules and regulations concerning the editing, publication, printing and distribution of books so as to bring about a vigorous development in this field of endeavour.

Education

In pre-liberation days over 80 per cent of China's population was illiterate, and the country was very backward in culture and education. Following the founding of the People's Republic in 1949, the government made the necessary structural changes in education. With the development of the national economy, the government has made great efforts to promote the development of socialist education, and remarkable progress has been obtained. By 1979 enrolment in the universities, colleges and secondary and primary schools totalled 207.94 million, or eight times the figure in the years immediately after liberation. Of this number, university and college students increased 8.7 times, secondary-school students 47.5 times, and primary-school pupils, 6 times. Spare-time and children's education and education for the blind and deaf-mutes have also made headway. Before the liberation, many minority nationalities had no schools. Now this backward situation in education has completely changed in the areas where they live in compact communities. By 1979, students of minority nationalities in schools at various levels totalled 9.54 million throughout the country, an increase of 9.6 times over 1951. This speed of growth far surpassed the level of average development in the nation.

In the thirty years (1949–79) after the birth of the new China, institutes of higher learning trained 3.03 million people with professional skills in various fields, and the secondary technical schools trained 5.39 million people for the state. These people have now become the foundation of the intellectual force in our country. The graduates of universities and secondary technical schools in the 1950s and 1960s, in particular, have become the backbone force in China's modernization drive today, now that they have had scores of years of practical experience. In addition, China's secondary agricultural schools, vocational schools and middle and primary schools have also trained and provided for the state a large reserve force of labour.

China's educational undertaking was seriously damaged during the Cultural Revolution. The quality in education dropped drastically, affecting a whole generation. After the country entered the new stage of socialist modernization, guided by the policy of readjustment, restructuring, consolidation and improvement, the educational undertaking was consolidated and readjusted, and reforms were introduced during the readjustment period. Fundamental changes have taken place on the educational front after years of hard work. There had been remarkable achievements by 1981, and a new situation had emerged throughout the country. (See Table 13.)

In 1981, there were 704 institutions of higher learning in the country. In 1982 about 298,000 students were enrolled in the colleges and universities, and the number of graduates was 139,600. The number of students now studying in these institutions of higher learning totals 1,279,500, an increase of 25.4 per cent over 1979 and 11.9 per cent over 1980. The teaching and administrative staff in these universities and colleges total 666,300, of which 249,900 are full-time teachers, 5,037 are professors, 21,421 are associate professors and 126,965 are lecturers.

During the readjustment of the educational undertakings, the needs of the various fields of construction have been taken into account, and attention has been paid to enrolling more students for the departments of finance and economics, political science and law, which have a weak foundation, thus bringing about a change in the proportion between the various departments in the universities and colleges. By 1980, the proportion of students studying finance and economics had risen to 3.2 per cent, as compared with 1.2 per cent in 1976. The proportion of students majoring in political science and law had risen to 0.5 per cent as against 0.1 per cent in 1976, and the proportion of students at teachers' colleges had risen from 19.4 per cent in 1976 to 29.6 per cent. All the scientific research set-ups in the universities and colleges had been restored, and new ones added. Fresh progress had been made in scientific research, and many items of research had attained a fairly high level with better economic results. They have contributed greatly to the development of China's science and technology and to the realization of the four modernizations.

To meet the needs of construction in the 1980s, the work of training

TABLE 13.　　　Basic situation of various kinds of schools in 1981

Type	Number of schools	Number of students (10,000)				Number of teaching and administrative staff (10,000)		Remarks
		Graduates	Students recruited	Total at school	Estimated graduates in 1982	Total	Full-time teachers	
				19 478.68 (20 534.88)		1 155.55	924.50	The total at school in the brackets includes children in kindergartens.
Higher learning	704	13.96	29.88	127.95	45.67	66.63	24.99	
Secondary	112 505	1 710.20	1 810.43	5 014.55	1 603.87	411.71	300.88	In the number of teaching and administrative staff of secondary schools, the teaching and administrative staff of schools run by the local people totalled 843 500.
Technical	3 132	60.49	43.32	106.90	44.60	32.57	13.59	
Specialized	2 170	36.48	23.81	63.21	24.18	24.89	9.84	
Normal	962	24.01	19.51	43.69	20.42	7.68	3.75	
General middle	106 718	1 640.29	1 740.45	4 859.56	1 545.01	374.54	284.40	
Senior middle	24 447	486.12	327.76	714.98	342.36	—	49.45	
Junior middle	82 271	1 154.17	1 412.69	4 144.58	1 202.65	—	234.95	
Agricultural and vocational	2 655	9.42	26.66	48.09	14.26	4.60	2.89	
Agricultural middle	2 094	7.75	14.96	26.78	8.33	2.99	1.74	
Vocational middle	561	1.67	11.70	21.31	5.93	1.61	1.15	
Primary	894 074	2 075.73	2 749.24	14 332.83	2 269.69	616.46	558.01	In the number of teaching and administrative staff of primary schools, the teaching and administrative staff of schools run by the local people totalled 3.36 million.
For the blind and deaf-mutes	302	0.37	0.60	3.35	—	0.86	0.51	
Kindergartens	130 296	—	—	1 056.20	—	59.89	40.11	

students in secondary technical schools was strengthened during the readjustment period. In 1981, there were 3,132 such schools in the country, 433,200 students were newly enrolled, 604,900 students graduated and the total number of students studying in these schools was 1,069,000. The teaching and administrative staff at the secondary technical schools throughout the country was 325,700, of which 135,900 were full-time teachers. Compared with 1980, the number of teaching and administrative staff had increased 10.1 per cent, and the number of full-time teachers had gone up by 6.7 per cent. In 1982, the secondary technical schools recruited 630,000 students, a considerable increase over the previous two years.

In order to raise the quality of secondary schools, appropriate readjustments have been made in the last few years, taking into consideration the fact that senior middle schools developed blindly during the ten chaotic years of the Cultural Revolution. This resulted in the unitary structure of the middle schools and a serious decline in educational quality. The scope for enrolling students in senior middle schools is now under control, while vigorous measures have been taken to develop secondary vocational and technical education. This is an important structural reform in China's secondary education. It is a principle that lays the stress on the reform of senior middle-school education, the simultaneous development of general education and vocational and technical education, and the setting up of schools by the state, relevant vocational departments, factories and mines, enterprises and people's communes. Education below the county level is geared mainly to the rural areas, serving the construction needs in these areas. The setting up of secondary vocational and technical schools by the various trades in the cities and countryside is encouraged; at the same time appropriate measures are taken to transform some senior middle schools into vocational-technical schools, secondary vocational schools or secondary agricultural schools. After readjustment and restructuring, in 1981 there were 106,700 general secondary schools with a total enrolment of 48,595,600 students in the country. Compared with 1979, the number of such schools had been cut by 37,500 and the number of students reduced by 21 per cent. Compared with 1980, the reduction was 11,700 schools and 6,485,200 students, of which the decrease in the number of senior middle school students was 26.3 per cent and the decrease in the number of junior middle school students was 8.7 per cent. On the other hand, vocational and technical education have developed accordingly. By 1981, there were 2,655 secondary vocational and agricultural schools in the country; that year 266,600 new students were enrolled, and the total number of students studying in these schools was 480,900. As regards the number of students at school, 1980 saw an increase of 93.1 per cent over the previous year, and 1981 again witnessed a further increase of 6 per cent. Of these, the increase in the number of students studying in the secondary vocational schools was 59.5 per cent. This shows that after the readjustment and restructuring of secondary education, the number of students in various kinds of vocational and technical schools has increased greatly in proportion as far as senior middle school education is concerned.

For primary schools, the focus is on further efforts to make primary education universal. In 1981, there were 894,100 primary schools in the country, 27,492,400 pupils were recruited, 20,757,300 graduated, and the total number of pupils at school was 143,328,300.

At present, 93 per cent of school-age children are studying in the primary schools. In order to popularize primary-school education more successfully, the distribution of primary schools in the rural areas has been readjusted in recent years in accordance with the principle of providing facilities for the children to go to the schools in nearby areas and using manpower and material resources sparingly. While making efforts to run the full-time primary schools well, attention has been paid to setting up various types of schools apart from the full-time ones, such as alternate-day schools, mobile schools and simply equipped schools, enabling more and more school-age children to have the chance of an education.

Kindergarten education, education for the blind and deaf-mutes and reformatories have received the attention and support of society at large. In 1981, there were 130,296 kindergartens in the country with a total of 10.562 million children. Schools for the blind and deaf-mutes numbered 302 in 1981, with an enrolment of 33,500. In the last two years, 23 provinces, municipalities and autonomous regions have set up 112 reformatories, with an enrolment of 7,200. Supported by various quarters of society and thanks to the hard work of staff members and teachers, there have been remarkable achievements in rescuing young people who committed offences against the law.

The government has always attached great importance to education for the minority nationalities. Since the founding of the People's Republic, the state has established the Central Institute for Nationalities in Beijing and nine other similar institutions of higher learning for the minority peoples in south-western, north-western and central-south China, and 100,000 minority people with professional skills of various kinds have been trained for the state. To train the people of the minority nationalities in a still better and quicker way for construction work in the areas where they live, the state educational administrative departments have taken appropriate measures, such as opening special classes for them in Qinghua University, Beijing University, Beijing Teachers' University and two other key universities in the country. Some institutions of higher learning in areas where the minority nationalities live in compact communities have also opened special classes and preparatory courses for students of the minority peoples. The national autonomous regions and the provinces with a large population of minority nationalities have drawn up plans to run normal schools so as to train more teachers for them. In 1980, there were 9,656,600 students of minority nationalities studying in various schools throughout the country, of which 42,900 were college students, 84,000 were students of secondary

88

specialized schools, 2,007,500 were students of secondary schools and 7,522,200 were pupils in primary schools.

As a result of China's socialist modernization, workers and peasants of all trades and professions and young educated people are enthusiastically studying science and culture. This situation has given an impetus to adult education. In 1981, there were 1,346,300 workers and peasants in various universities and colleges, of which 268,000 were studying in radio and television universities, 491,000 in universities and colleges for workers and peasants and 587,300 were middle-school teachers taking a refresher course. In the same year, there were 8,206,700 worker-peasant students receiving an intermediate education. Among them, 3,118,600 were studying in secondary technical and agricultural schools (1,964,600 were workers of enterprises or factories and 1,154,000 were peasants), 3,766,400 were studying in spare-time secondary schools (workers and staff members numbered 3,132,500 and peasants, 633,900); 1,321,700 were primary-school teachers taking a refresher course. There were 9,735,600 worker-peasant students in spare-time primary schools. Last year, 3,538,700 people took lessons in literacy classes. (See Table 14.)

Practice in past years has proved that university- and college-run correspondence courses and evening courses (which constitute the main part of higher education for workers and peasants) have contributed greatly to the development of adult education. The educational administrative departments in China have decided that when students taking college correspondence courses or specialized correspondence courses or studying at evening universities have completed their studies and passed the examinations, they should be given diplomas by the institutions of higher learning concerned. Graduates of correspondence courses and evening courses run by universities and colleges that have the right to confer academic degrees may confer such diplomas in accordance with state stipulations.

The work of sending students to study abroad or receiving foreign students to study in China is also being actively undertaken. In the last three years, 5,609 students have been sent to study in 46 countries, and 1,276 students from 79 countries have come to study in China. Many foreign experts and scholars have also been invited to come and lecture. Educational delegations and investigation groups have been sent abroad to study and attend important international academic conferences. Since joining Unesco, China has played its role in promoting mutual understanding, unity and friendship.

China's education is socialist in character. The policy of its socialist schools is to enable everyone who receives an education to develop morally, intellectually and physically and to uphold the principle of 'being both red and expert', that is both socialist-minded and vocationally proficient. They should be labourers with a good education and able builders in the work of socialist modernization. Schools of various types and levels should all consider teaching as the key link and continually raise the quality of education.

TABLE 14. Basic situation of worker-peasant education at various levels in 1981, unit: 10 000

Type	Graduates	Students recruited	Number of students at school			Teaching and administrative staff	
			Total	Workers and staff members	Peasants	Total	Full-time teachers
Total			1 928.86	844.16	1 084.70	47.92	37.19
Worker-peasant education in institutions of higher learning	31.53	17.11	134.63	134.17	0.46	10.71	5.61
Radio and TV universities	4.76	—	26.80	26.80	—	1.49	0.65
Worker-peasant schools of higher learning	7.57	17.11	49.10	48.64	0.46	3.23	1.71
Colleges (schools) for middle-school teachers' advanced studies	19.20		58.73	58.73	—	5.99	3.25
Secondary education for workers and peasants	173.35	319.06	820.67	641.88	178.79	11.98	8.52
Secondary technical schools for workers and peasants	71.98	143.10	311.86	196.46	115.40	5.07	3.63
Spare-time middle schools	75.47	247.96	376.64	313.25	63.39	6.91	4.89
Schools for primary-school teachers' advanced studies	25.90		132.17	132.17	—	—	—
Spare-time elementary education for workers and peasants	421.64	571.53	973.56	68.11	905.45	25.23	23.06
Classes of spare-time primary schools	67.77	198.78	352.29	47.26	305.03		
Literacy classes	353.87	372.75	621.27	20.85	600.12		

The number of teaching and administrative staff of colleges for middle school teachers' advanced studies includes the number of teachers and staff members of schools for primary-school teachers' advanced studies.

The Ministry of Education is a government organization under the State Council, in charge of leading and administering the country's educational affairs as well as being an administrative organ in implementing the socialist policies and principles of education. Educational administrations have been established in all the provinces, municipalities, autonomous regions, prefectures and counties. China's educational undertaking implements the principle of combining unity with diversification, popularization with the raising of standards, and planning by the central authorities with management by the localities and departments at various levels. Encouragement is given to schools which are simultaneously full-time, part-work and part-study, and leisure-time schools; simultaneous development of general and vocational (technical) education; simultaneous promotion of adult and children's education; and simultaneous development of school, TV, broadcasting and correspondence education.

The policy of dual leadership and leadership by departments concerned is implemented with regard to universities and colleges in China. The Ministry of Education and educational departments in the various provinces, municipalities and autonomous regions exercise leadership over the comprehensive universities, polytechnic colleges and teachers' universities and colleges, while departments concerned at the central, provincial, municipal, and autonomous regional levels are mainly in charge of engineering, agricultural, medical, financial and economic, art, physical culture and sports institutions of higher education. Secondary technical schools are under the dual administration of the professional departments concerned and educational administrations, with stress on the former. Secondary and primary schools are under the administration of the various provinces, municipalities and autonomous regions; those in the cities are under the leadership of the city or district educational administrations, while those in the rural areas are primarily under the county educational administrations or the people's communes and production brigades.

In order to raise the educational level so as to train quickly people with professional skills, to give them the experience needed and play an exemplary role for other schools, a number of key universities, secondary technical schools and secondary and primary schools are being run by the central authorities and the various provinces, municipalities and autonomous regions.

At present China's educational work still cannot meet the needs of the modernization of agriculture, industry, national defence and science and technology. Educational administrative organizations at various levels, on the basis of their achievements, will continue to implement the policy of readjustment, restructuring, consolidation and improvement, and work hard for the sound development of China's education.

The press and broadcasting

In the new historical period, an excellent situation prevails in the press and broadcasting, with conspicuous improvements both in content and form, and in quantity and quality.

For the Chinese press, 1980 was a year of great development. More than 230 newspapers (36 at the central level, 152 at the provincial, municipal and autonomous regional level, and 42 at the county level) were published and distributed throughout the country, with a total circulation of 14,056 million copies.

Renmin Ribao (People's Daily) is the organ of the Central Committee of the Chinese Communist Party and the most important newspaper in China. Every day it communicates to the nation and the world the principles and policies of the party and the People's Government, publishes major news on China and the world, comments on and discusses ideological and theoretical questions, introduces experiences in work and the new socialist ideas that have emerged across the nation. It publishes eight pages every day and is distributed in 123 countries as well as Xianggang (Hong Kong) and Aomen (Macao).

Other newspapers in China include: *Guangming Ribao* (Brightness Daily) which is mainly for intellectuals working in the cultural, educational, scientific and technical fields; *Gongren Ribao* (Workers' Daily); *Zhongguo Nongmin Bao* (China Peasants' Paper) and *Zhongguo Caimao Bao* (China Financial and Trade Journal) mainly intended for those employed in finance and trade. They have a large circulation, ranging from hundreds of thousands to over a million copies each. In addition, there are *Zhongguo Qingnian Bao* (Chinese Youth News) with a circulation of 3.1 million copies and *Zhongguo Shaonian Bao* (Chinese Children's Paper), which is referred to as the bosom friend of the hundreds of millions of Chinese children, both having a circulation of 10.3 million copies per issue. There are also papers in specialized fields, including *Tiyu Bao* (Sports Journal), *Jiankang Bao* (Health Journal), *Shichang* (Market), *Zhongguo Fazhi Bao* (China's Legal System Journal) and *Tuanjie Bao* (Unity). In some big cities evening newspapers are published. All this testifies to the flourishing state of the Chinese press.

Energetic efforts made in recent years to improve China's journalistic work have been rewarded with encouraging success. For example, *Renmin Ribao* formerly contained only six pages a day, but now has eight pages with emphasis on economic news and reports. Its news reports are not only authentic but also timely and concise. It is worthy of particular notice that critical news articles are also published in China's newspapers. This is an expression of the spirit of socialist democracy and has won the admiration of the people. Many newspapers have taken on a new look, characterized by their diversified special columns and liveliness, attractive illustrations and vividly written articles. Newspapers in the capital alone have opened up about fifty special columns; the contents are lively and of great interest and the language is terse and clear. These papers are all well received by the readers.

China has two news agencies: Xinhua News Agency and the China News Agency.

Xinhua is a government news agency with more than 7,000 reporters. It has branch offices in all the provinces (excluding Taiwan), municipalities and autonomous regions. In addition it has branches in 85 countries and regions with 150 correspondents stationed abroad. Xinhua releases domestic and international news every day for the home press, and sends out domestic and international news in English, French, Spanish, Arabic and Russian to all parts of the world. News items are also broadcast abroad through the English programme as well as the special programmes in English, French, Spanish, Arabic and Russian. The daily newscast in the five languages runs to 150,000 words. Xinhua News Agency also publishes daily news bulletins in six languages—Chinese, English, French, Spanish, Arabic and Russian.

The China News Agency is run by the people. Founded on 1 October 1952, it is managed by a board of directors composed of patriotic personalities from various circles. Based in Beijing, it has branch offices in Guangdong and Fujian Provinces and in Shanghai. It also has reporters stationed in Guangxi and Yunnan, and an office in Xianggang. It sends out news dispatches, articles, special features and photos to newspapers published in Chinese abroad and in Xianggang and Aomen. Apart from this, it distributes films abroad on China's landscape, cultural relics, construction and local operas.

China's radio and television are under the leadership of the Ministry of Radio and Television. The various provinces, municipalities, prefectures and counties have special structures to take charge of the work of radio and TV stations and a radio rediffusion network. A comprehensive broadcasting system has been developed, beamed to various parts of China and the rest of the world, TV is transmitted to different parts of the country and a radio rediffusion network exists in the rural areas. The state radio and TV stations and technical departments directly under the Ministry of Radio and Television have established business connections with their counterparts in seventy countries and regions, in addition to links with nine relevant international organizations. The Central Television Station has established tele-cine business exchange relations with TV stations in twenty countries and regions and has signed agreements of co-operation in radio and TV broadcasting with some countries.

By 1980, China had 106 radio stations, 484 transmission and relay stations, and 2,560 rediffusion stations. At present, it adopts mainly amplitude modulation in broadcasting, using medium and short wave frequencies. The Central People's Broadcasting Station has two comprehensive broadcasting programmes for the whole nation, one for the minority nationalities, one for Taiwan and one using FM for broadcasting music. Radio stations in the various provinces, municipalities and autonomous regions have a total of 130 broadcast programmes.

Using thirty-eight foreign languages and Chinese (the 'Common Speech' and four local dialects), China broadcasts news items and articles on China's politics, economy, culture and social life to promote friendship and understanding between the people of China and the rest of the world.

In the last few years, the Central Broadcasting Station has made some changes with respect to its newscasts, altering the situation in which it depended mainly on newspapers and news agencies for news. In 1980, 40 per cent of its broadcasts on home news were contributed by its own reporters. The proportion is much larger for radio stations in the various provinces, municipalities and autonomous regions, sometimes accounting for 80 to 90 per cent of the total. News items contributed by their own reporters enjoy great popularity for they are timely, short and fresh. This is particularly so with tape-recorded news items, which are more appealing and give the audiences the feeling they are really on the scene.

Art and theatrical items occupy a large proportion of the broadcasts. For instance, in the case of the Central Broadcasting Station's Programme One, art and theatrical items, including music, operas, novels, radio plays, film recordings, modern dramas and items selected by the audience themselves, account for about 60 per cent of the total. To satisfy music lovers, the Central Broadcasting Station and the radio stations in Shanghai, Heilongjiang, Hebei, Hunan and other places use FM to broadcast music for better effect.

China's television has made great progress since it was started in 1958. There are stations in the nation's twenty-nine provinces, municipalities and autonomous regions (the station in Tibet is being constructed). The Central TV Station and an increasing number of local stations have started colour transmission. To date, there are in China 38 central TV stations, 246 TV transmission-relaying stations with a capacity of over 1,000 kW, and over 2,000 smaller relay stations. Over the past two years, television plays have developed rapidly. In 1980 and 1981, more than 250 were produced and broadcast whereas in 1979 there were only 40. Together with the organizations concerned, the Central TV Station carried out in 1980 and 1981 national selections of the best TV plays; twenty-eight plays were awarded prizes in 1980 and ten in 1981. Among them are: *Trifles of the Ordinary People, Girlfriends, At the Wedding Chamber, Good Uncles* (for children), *The Other Side, Deep Love of the Earth, Girls Selling Flatbreads, Parents and Their Children.* With varied subject-matter, they have won approval from the general public. Some of these plays reflect life on the industrial and agricultural front and in the army, some reflect the world outlook and the happy life of the young people, others depict how the less advanced are helped to improve ideologically, or portray children's life and mirror socialist ethics and trends.

94

Radio and television have contributed also to training the young people and helping them acquire knowledge. The Central People's Broadcasting Station runs a TV university, which in 1980 enrolled its second batch of students, bringing the total number to 420,000 in two years. There were, of course, many more students who had not been able to enrol. The university teaches sixteen subjects in a course of three years. In the first two school years, it gave courses on higher mathematics, general physics, theory of mechanics, mechanics of materials, organic chemistry, circuit principles and English. A TV education network has thus been formed from the central level to the localities. In addition, the Central TV Station also sponsors lectures on twelve subjects including electronic computers and fundamentals of semi-conductor circuits. In some provinces and municipalities, the radio and TV stations run courses for secondary-school students. Such education has played a very important role in helping the people study science and culture.

Radio and TV are playing an increasingly big role in the cultural life of the Chinese people. There are, however, many problems that have to be solved in order to enable them to serve the people still better.

Cultural relics

China has a long history and a splendid ancient culture created by the people of the various nationalities in the country. The cultural heritage is rich indeed. However, in the semi-feudal and semi-colonial China, there were no special institutions in charge of protecting cultural relics, large quantities of which were plundered by the foreign invaders or smuggled out of the country. Many ancient structures were in disrepair, damaged by the elements or destroyed by plunderers. Since the founding of the new China, the people have become masters of the nation's historical relics. The People's Government has promulgated a series of laws and decrees and taken concrete administrative measures to protect these relics and to prevent them from being smuggled out of the country. Thus, an end has been put to the destruction that has been going on for nearly a century. The protection of the heritage is now undertaken on a scale unknown before, thereby ushering in a socialist new era for cultural relics.

The Administration Bureau of Cultural Relics under the Ministry of Culture is in charge of the work of protecting and managing the cultural heritage. Corresponding organizations are set up in the various provinces, municipalities and autonomous regions. Under the Chinese Academy of Social Sciences there is the Archaeological Research Institute engaged, as its name denotes, in research work on cultural relics and in archaeology.

It is the consistent policy of the Chinese Government to protect cultural relics. In the thirty-four years since the founding of the People's Republic of China, this work has progressed along with the development of economic

95

construction. During the ten-year Cultural Revolution, beginning in 1966, however, the work met with severe interference, resulting in serious damage to the cultural heritage. Institutions in charge of relics in many places were disbanded, and the work of protection came to a standstill. With the concern and support of the beloved Premier Zhou Enlai (Chou En Lai), China's archaeological workers resisted the interference of the Gang of Four and did much work under very difficult conditions. In the new historical period, cultural relics work has recommenced and is forging ahead again. Many ancient buildings, grottoes and revolutionary memorial buildings have been repaired and opened to visitors, both domestic and foreign. There have also been many new archaeological finds. The State Council has issued a new decree on the protection of cultural relics, enabling this undertaking to develop in depth and in scope.

Experience has proved that making a general survey of the distribution of China's cultural relics and organizing the cultural relics protection units are important measures in ensuring success. By 'cultural relics protection units' we mean the groups concerned with relics which cannot and should not be moved but should be kept in their original place. These fall mainly under two categories: (a) ancient relics, including architecture, grottoes, stone carvings, sites and tombs, and (b) modern relics, including revolutionary sites and revolutionary memorial buildings. The measures consist of making a strict appraisal before putting relics under the care of special organizations at various levels. In other words, the cultural relics are carefully selected and clearly defined as items for protection at the provincial, municipal and autonomous regional level in accordance with their value on the basis of the general survey already made. Local governments have successively made known a number of their own cultural relics preservation items, and the State Council, after an appraisal, makes those items that are of particular value and importance the national key preservation items. The names of the key items for protection were made known in 1961 and in 1982, totalling 242 in all. Table 15 gives the relics listed for protection.

The 'cultural relics protection units' at various levels enjoy the protection of China's Constitution. The government has set up special administrations or research organizations to protect these key cultural relics. For instance, museums, research institutes or protection offices have been set up to protect and look after particularly important cultural relics, such as the Palace Museum and the Dunhuang and Longmen grottoes. According to the stipulations of government decrees, the local governments at various levels have the responsibility of doing a good job in protecting the relics. For each 'cultural relics protection unit' the protection area should be clearly defined. With regard to the ancient structures, memorial buildings and grottoes, not only should they be kept intact, but a definite area all round them should be protected so that they will remain as they were in the past. The planning and designing of new buildings around them should

TABLE 15.   National key cultural relics protection items

Items	First batch (made known in 1961)	Second batch (made known in 1982)
Revolutionary sites and revolutionary memorial structures	33	10
Grottoes	14	5
Ancient architecture and historical memorial buildings	77	28
Stone carvings and others	11	2
Ancient sites	26	10
Ancient tombs	19	7
TOTAL	180	62

be in harmony with the surroundings and atmosphere. In the case of ancient sites and tombs, besides determining the area for protection, the treasures discovered underground are also made key protection zones. Signboards with the names of the 'cultural relics protection units' should be put up. On these boards are written the names of the organizations that have announced their decision to protect these relics, the date of the announcement, the class to which these relics belong, their history, art and scientific value. There are archives with scientific records and data for research work as well as material concerning protection, repair, restoration and excavation—historical documents, written records, rubbings, photos and charts. There are professional people and organizations in charge of the day-to-day work of protection and management. Funds needed for the preservation of these cultural relics, archaeological excavations and repair of the ancient structures are all listed in the financial budgets of various local authorities and are guaranteed by the state.

To protect certain cities that are extremely rich in cultural relics or are of great historical and revolutionary significance, the State Council has, after careful examination and evaluation, named these cities 'renowned historical and cultural cities'. Comprehensive plans have been drawn up for their reconstruction and management so that their special features may be maintained.

An important aspect in the work of protecting cultural relics is the investigation, repair and study of the grottoes and ancient architecture.

Investigation of the grottoes started in the early years of the People's Republic. In 1951, for instance, specialists were organized to make an all-round investigation of the Mogao Grottoes of Dunhuang. This was followed by planned and fairly thorough surveys conducted in Gansu, Sichuan, Yunnan, Henan, Hebei, Shanxi, Shandong, Jiangsu, Zhejiang, Inner Mongolia and Tibet. Documentary records relating to the grottoes were compiled on the basis of these investigations. Preliminary appraisals of the age of some grottoes were made and many-sided studies on special subjects were carried out. To prevent erosion and other damage, some key grottoes were repaired. This includes, for instance, the reinforcing of the rocky walls of the Mogao Grottoes of Dunhuang. Projects to protect the grottoes of Yungang and Longmen from collapse and weathering were carried out. In the case of the Maijishan Grottoes in Gansu, the reinforcement project was coupled with the repair of an ancient plank road built along the face of the cliff, which reconnects the grottoes in the eastern and the western parts of the cliff and which had collapsed about 1,200 years ago. This makes it possible for people to visit the grottoes, which were not accessible previously.

Remarkable progress has also been made with respect to the protection of the ancient architecture. Built mainly of wood, these ancient buildings are known throughout the world for their complete and intricate systems and unique styles. Of the first batch of 180 national key cultural relics protection items, made known in 1961, there are seventy-seven ancient structures, accounting for 43 per cent of the total. Of the cultural relics listed for protection at the provincial, municipal and autonomous regional level, about half are ancient buildings. In the past few years, much repair work has been done in accordance with the principle of 'maintaining their present state or restoring them to their original form'. According to incomplete statistics, close to a thousand ancient buildings have been repaired on a large scale. They include the world-famous Zhaozhou Stone Bridge, the Fuguang Monastery on Mount Wutai, The Longxin Monastery in Hebei, the Jin Monastery in Shanxi and the Beihai Park and Ming Tombs in Beijing which have undergone large-scale repairs and are now well preserved. The state has also made all-round plans to repair some groups of large buildings, such as the Palace Museum in Beijing and the Mountain Summer Resort in Chengde. The moving of the Yongle Palace of the Yuan Dynasty is one of the largest repair projects undertaken since the founding of the new China.

Many important ancient structures have been discovered in the course of the general survey and the re-examination of the cultural relics conducted after the founding of the People's Republic. Six stone structures of the Han Dynasty have been discovered, including an ancient palace, temples and graveyards and structures in and around them. Valuable wooden structures have also been discovered ranging from those built in the Tang Dynasty to those built in the Yuan Dynasty. In addition, many houses of the ancient people have been discovered. In 1980, for instance, more than 130 Ming structures were discovered in Jingdezhen in Jiangxi Province, including the dwelling houses of the people, ancestral halls, gates of alleys and shops. Especially valuable is the discovery of an 80-metre-long complete Ming-dynasty street in Shenlumiao Street of Jingdezhen. The ancient structures of various dynasties existing today serve as a valuable textbook on the history of the development of Chinese architecture.

Another important task is to carry out archaeological investigations and excavations in co-ordination with national economic construction. This work is under the unified leadership of the Administration Bureau of Cultural Relics under the Ministry of Culture and the Chinese Academy of Social Sciences with the approval of the government. After the founding of the new China, investigations and excavations were carried out throughout the country, and abundant data and materials were found to complete the knowledge of that part of Chinese history for which no written records existed. For instance, there have been new discoveries of Peking Man fossils along with stone artefacts and ashes, the skulls and mandibles of the Lantian Man in Lantian of Shaanxi Province (more primitive than the Peking Man) together with stone artefacts dating back 600,000 years. The Yuanmou Man dating back 1.7 million years was discovered in Yunnan Province in south-western China. In addition, Palaeolithic remains have also been discovered in Jilin, Inner Mongolia, Ningxia, Henan, Shanxi, Sichuan, Hubei, Guangdong, Guangxi and the Qinghai-Tibet Plateau. These discoveries have provided clues for the study of the evolution of the culture and natural environment of human beings in the Palaeolithic period. They have extended the area of the culture of primitive man in China and provided important materials for the study of geology, palaeogeography and palaeometeorology.

Neolithic remains have also been discovered all over the country. According to incomplete statistics, there are 6,000 sites, which have filled in the blanks in knowledge regarding areas and ages. The newly discovered Peiligang culture in Xinzhen of Henan Province and the Cishan culture in Cishan of Wuan, Hebei Province, dating back 8,000 years, are of great value to the study of the culture of the Upper Neolithic Period in China. These discoveries show that in the vast Chinese territory there were various cultures in the Neolithic period which reflected different sources of development and which, through interflow and mutual influence, gradually united. This is of great significance in the study of the formation of the Chinese nation.

There have been new and extremely important archaeological discoveries from China's three earliest dynasties—Xia, Shang and Zhou—and the later Song, Yuan and Ming dynasties. Valuable cultural relics have been unearthed from the sites of the historical capitals and ancient tombs, which graphically reflect, from different angles, the social systems, politics, economy and culture as well as the social life of those periods. Especially in the last few years, many rare objects have been discovered, such as the jade burial suit sewn with fine gold wire unearthed from a Western Han tomb in Mancheng of Hebei Province, the 'Bronze Galloping Horses' in Wuwei of Gansu Province, a silk painting from a Western Han tomb at Mawangdui in Changsha, the life-size terracotta warriors and horses unearthed east of the Qin Shi Huang Tomb in Lintong of Shaanxi Province, 'Sun Bin's Art of Military Law' from a Han tomb in Linyi of Shandong

Province which had been lost for many years, bamboo slips inscribed with the laws of the Qin Dynasty unearthed in Xiaogan of Hubei Province, and a bronze bell and exquisite bronze vessels from a tomb in Hubei Province. In the last few years, Chinese cultural and archaeological workers, using archaeological methods, have made investigations into the historical changes of the rivers, sea coasts and deserts, and they have had some success in opening up a new realm of archaeology.

'Making the past serve the present' is the principle guiding China's work on cultural relics. To spread historical and cultural knowledge among the broad masses of the people and to educate them in patriotism, all the archaeological finds, after being scientifically examined and studied, have been exhibited in local museums. According to the decrees governing cultural relics, the Administration Bureau of Cultural Relics under the Ministry of Culture has the right to requisition the cultural relics unearthed in the various localities and entrust them to the care of specific organizations. Most of the exhibits in the Chinese History Hall of the Museum of Chinese History in Beijing are from various places in the country. Exhibits of local museums are mostly relics unearthed locally, in addition to those in the original collection. The most important cultural relics are put on display in various parts of the country.

Since 1973, China has organized exhibitions of cultural relics in many friendly countries to promote mutual understanding.

At present, Chinese cultural-relics workers are doing their best to enable these relics to play a bigger role in raising the scientific and cultural level of the Chinese nation as a whole and to contribute to the realization of the four modernizations.

Titles in this series:

The serial numbering of titles in this series, the presentation of which has been
modified, was discontinued with the volume *Cultural policy in Italy*

[II] CLT.83/XIX.76/A